Leadership as Performance

Leadership as Performance: Developing Leadership Skills through Acting is based on the premise that leadership is a performance, a role played by leaders to inspire followers to achieve a shared goal. The book explores how acting techniques can facilitate the development of leadership skills. For this purpose, it introduces the SPACE model of leadership development, which is based on five key leadership skills: self-awareness, presence, authenticity, communication, and emotional intelligence.

The book is divided into three parts. The first part explores the metaphor of leadership as a performance and the fundamentals of both leadership and acting. The second part elaborates on the SPACE model by showing how each of the five key leadership skills can be developed with acting techniques. The final part explores how improvisation can help leaders adapt to change, work with teams, and foster creativity and innovation. It also discusses the role of visionary leadership in inspiring others and creating a shared purpose. Readers are provided with tools to build on their skills through a range of pedagogy, including a set of self-reflective questions in each chapter, acting-based exercises and improvisations in the most practical chapters, and discussions of cases of well-known leaders.

This book is ideal for leaders, practitioners, and students interested in exploring how to develop leadership skills through acting. It is an excellent read for undergraduate and graduate leadership courses as well as executive education programs.

Marco Aponte-Moreno is a Professor of Clinical Management and Organization at the University of Southern California's Marshall School of Business in Los Angeles. He is also a trained actor with over 25 years of acting experience.

Leadership as Performance
Developing Leadership Skills
through Acting

Marco Aponte-Moreno

Routledge
Taylor & Francis Group
LONDON AND NEW YORK

Designed cover image: [©Getty Images Creative #:179311336]

First published 2025

by Routledge
4 Park Square, Milton Park, Abingdon, Oxon OX14 4RN

and by Routledge
605 Third Avenue, New York, NY 10158

Routledge is an imprint of the Taylor & Francis Group, an informa business

British Library Cataloguing-in-Publication Data
A catalogue record for this book is available from the British Library

ISBN: 9781032394602 (hbk)
ISBN: 9781032394626 (pbk)
ISBN: 9781003349815 (ebk)

DOI: 10.4324/9781003349815

Typeset in Sabon
by Deanta Global Publishing Services, Chennai, India

Contents

For Hurley

Preface

In 1997, while working for the French bank Crédit Lyonnais in New York City, I stumbled upon a speech class for actors at the HB Studio, a well-established theater school in Greenwich Village. This class changed my life. Although I was not an actor, the instructor, Ruth Berkowitz, allowed me to take the class after I insisted that I needed to take it because of how frustrated I was with my foreign accent.

I didn't like my accent, a mix of sounds between Spanish from Venezuela, where I was born and raised, and French from Paris, where I attended college. I felt my accent was affecting my work in general, and especially my chances of getting promoted at the bank. Also, I wanted to reduce my accent so that I could sound more "American." I wanted to fit in.

I took the speech class almost every semester for five years. After countless drills and repetitions, I ended up improving my accent and diction. And although I didn't completely lose my accent, people were able to understand me well. I didn't have to repeat my sentences in conversations for others to clearly understand what I was saying.

During those five years, out of curiosity, I began taking other classes at the studio including acting technique, scene study, and improvisation. Little by little, without even realizing it, I developed a love for acting and theater. Eventually, I became an actor. Well, more of a part-time actor, because I continued working in the field of business, first as a banker and then as a professor of leadership and management.

Over the past 20 years, I have performed in dozens of plays and short films. I even had a small role in the feature film *Hugo* directed by Martin Scorsese in 2011. In all these years pursuing both fields, I have realized that the benefits that leaders can get from acting go far beyond improving speech and diction. Acting can help develop self-awareness, presence, authenticity, communication, and empathy. It can help us, as leaders, in our efforts to lead teams, to understand and embrace diversity, and especially to motivate, influence, and inspire others. This is the premise of this book: that the qualities and techniques used by actors on stage can be utilized to develop the essential skills and qualities necessary for effective leadership.

As an actor and professor of leadership, I am fascinated by the intersection of these two fields. While some might see acting and leadership as distinct disciplines, I have come to realize that they are intimately related, both requiring the ability to connect with and inspire others. My passion for acting and leadership has led me to explore the ways in which acting can complement and reinforce leadership. This book is the culmination of many years of thinking about the connection between these two fields. It is based on the metaphor that leadership is a performance, a role played by leaders to inspire followers to achieve a shared goal.

By examining the parallels between leadership and acting, I hope to offer you a fresh perspective on leadership development, so that you can explore how acting techniques can be applied to enhance your own leadership abilities and those of others.

Acknowledgments

This book has been a collaborative effort involving the support, guidance, and expertise of many individuals and organizations. I am deeply grateful to each and every one of them.

First of all, I would like to thank the theaters where I have had the opportunity to train and act, especially the HB Studio in New York, Theatro Technis in London, and the Santa Monica Playhouse in Los Angeles. These venues have provided me with invaluable opportunities to develop my acting skills and gain a deeper understanding of the art of performance.

I am also grateful to the Marshall School of Business at the University of Southern California, where I am privileged to teach leadership to the next generation of business leaders. My colleagues at USC have provided me with a supportive and stimulating environment in which to develop and refine my ideas about leadership development. Special thanks to my colleague, Kirstin Eggers, for inspiring me to learn more about improvisation. Gratitude is also extended to my students, who have been a constant source of inspiration and learning throughout my career. Your insights, questions, and challenges have helped to shape my thinking about leadership and acting, and have kept me engaged and energized in my work.

I also extend my thanks to Alexandra McGregor, Holly Martin, and the entire team at Routledge and the Taylor & Francis Group for their invaluable perspectives in the book's evolution.

To my dear husband, Lance, the most intelligent man I know: your endless curiosity, sharp critical thinking, and vast knowledge have inspired me not only in writing this book but also in everything I have accomplished in all our years together.

Finally, I want to dedicate this book to my son Hurley. Your capacity to care for others, to create beautiful art, and to adapt and overcome life challenges are an inspiration not only for me, but for all those who know you well. Your love is the greatest gift I have ever received. Without you, this book would have not been possible.

Part I

Setting the stage

In his essay "Leadership as a Performing Art," American academic Warren Bennis, a pioneer of modern leadership studies, famously remarked that "leadership is not just a performing art, it may be the greatest performing art of all."[1] For Bennis, leadership is an art that requires creativity, intuition, and improvisation. He argues that effective leadership is closer to the work of a musician or a dancer than to the work of a scientist or an engineer.

Bennis suggests that like a performer, a leader must be able to read the mood and energy of the audience (the followers) and adjust their performance (leadership style) accordingly. This requires a great deal of self-awareness, empathy, and flexibility. Bennis also emphasizes the importance of authenticity in leadership, suggesting that effective leaders must have a clear sense of their own identity and values, and be willing to express them in their leadership role. In this sense, leadership is not just about achieving specific goals or objectives, but also about expressing a deeper sense of purpose and meaning.

This book builds upon Bennis' comparison by delving into the fundamentals of leadership as performance and examining how acting techniques can be utilized to enhance leadership abilities. Through this exploration, you will gain fresh perspectives on leadership development and a deeper understanding of how acting techniques can be applied to cultivate essential leadership skills.

Note

1 Bennis, W. G., & Biederman, P. W. (2015). *The Essential Bennis* (p. 341). Jossey-Bass.

DOI: 10.4324/9781003349815-1

1 Leadership as performance

Gustavo Dudamel, the renowned Venezuelan conductor of the Los Angeles Philharmonic, once said, "When people feel that something really special is happening on the stage, things change."[1] This statement, which he made during an interview after his 2011 London concert at the BBC Proms, captures the capacity that performance has to transform an audience.

As a conductor, Dudamel is known for bringing a strong sense of collective purpose to every performance. He creates a communion between the director, the musicians, and the audience. Joshua Kosman of the *San Francisco Chronicle* writes that Dudamel "brings a kinetic vitality to the music that can be impossible to resist."[2] His passion for music is infectious and has the capacity to inspire his musicians and audiences alike. His exceptional talent and ability to energize his musicians and captivate audiences demonstrate how performance can be a powerful force to unite, inspire, and transform people. Through his exceptional leadership and vision as a conductor, Dudamel has transformed the classical music world.

Leadership is a performance, resembling that of a director like Dudamel. It requires a combination of skills, qualities, and actions that are performed in a deliberate and intentional manner to achieve a desired outcome. At its core, leadership involves guiding and inspiring others toward a common goal or objective. Just like a performer, the leader must present a clear vision and articulate it effectively to their followers. They must be able to convey the mission, values, and purpose of the organization in a way that inspires others to follow. This requires excellent communication skills, including active listening, empathy, and the ability to tailor communication to different audiences.

DOI: 10.4324/9781003349815-2

In a performance, the audience responds to the performer's energy, enthusiasm, and passion. Similarly, in leadership, a leader's energy, enthusiasm, and passion can be contagious and motivate their team to take action. A leader must be able to set the tone for the team and create a positive and productive work environment. Just like a performer, a leader must be aware of their audience and adjust their style accordingly. Different situations call for different types of leadership. For example, a crisis may require a more directive top-down style of leadership, while a creative project may require a more collaborative approach. A good leader can adapt their leadership style to the situation, the team, and the desired outcome.

But leadership, like good performances, requires preparation and practice. Stage actors rehearse for weeks before opening night. In leadership, this means spending time developing the necessary skills and knowledge to effectively lead a team. This includes developing expertise in the field, honing one's own leadership skills, building a strong network, and seeking out mentorship and coaching.

Many famous leaders have recognized the strong connection between leadership and performance. Steve Jobs, the late co-founder of Apple, was known for his theatrical presentations and attention to detail when launching new products. He understood the power of showmanship and creating an emotional connection with his audience. Similarly, Winston Churchill, the former British prime minister, was a masterful orator who used his speeches to inspire and rally his country during times of crisis. He recognized that his words and delivery could impact the morale and determination of his people.

In his book *Onward: How Starbucks Fought for Its Life without Losing Its Soul*,[3] Howard Schultz, the former CEO of Starbucks who is known for his charismatic and passionate leadership, writes, "Leadership is like theater, and you're always on stage. You have to be authentic, you have to be real, and you have to be able to communicate in a way that moves people."

In recent years, the connection between leadership and performance is receiving more and more attention. Top business schools have been incorporating leadership development courses and workshops in their curricula for some time now. At the USC Marshall Business School, for example, graduate and undergraduate students have the option of taking an elective on leadership and improvisation. The same is true for many other business schools in the United States and abroad. As stated by Howard Schultz, effective leadership involves performance. Leaders' ability to inspire, motivate, and create a lasting impact can be achieved through deliberate and intentional performances, much like actors do on stage.

All the world's a stage

William Shakespeare's idea that life is a theater is a recurring theme in his plays and sonnets. It is a metaphor that suggests that the world is a stage, and that humans are actors who play different roles throughout their lives. This metaphor highlights the performative aspect of human behavior, suggesting that we are always "on stage," and that our lives are a kind of drama or play.

One of the most famous expressions of this idea can be found in the play *As You Like It*,[4] where the character Jaques delivers the famous monologue that begins with the lines "All the world's a stage, And all the men and women merely players." In this monologue, Jaques compares the different stages of human life to different acts in a play, highlighting the idea that we are all performing different roles throughout our lives:

All the world's a stage,
And all the men and women merely players;
They have their exits and their entrances;
And one man in his time plays many parts,
His acts being seven ages. At first the infant,
Mewling and puking in the nurse's arms;
And then the whining school-boy, with his satchel
And shining morning face, creeping like snail
Unwillingly to school. And then the lover,
Sighing like furnace, with a woeful ballad
Made to his mistress' eyebrow. Then a soldier,
Full of strange oaths, and bearded like the pard,
Jealous in honour, sudden and quick in quarrel,
Seeking the bubble reputation
Even in the cannon's mouth. And then the justice,
In fair round belly with good capon lin'd,

With eyes severe and beard of formal cut,
Full of wise saws and modern instances;
And so he plays his part. The sixth age shifts
Into the lean and slipper'd pantaloon,
With spectacles on nose and pouch on side;
His youthful hose, well sav'd, a world too wide
For his shrunk shank; and his big manly voice,
Turning again toward childish treble, pipes
And whistles in his sound. Last scene of all,
That ends this strange eventful history,
Is second childishness and mere oblivion;
Sans teeth, sans eyes, sans taste, sans everything.

Another Shakespearean play where this idea is explored is *Hamlet*.[5] In this play, the character Hamlet frequently makes references to the theater, suggesting that life is like a play. In Act 3, Scene 2, for example, Hamlet reflects on the actor's ability to evoke emotions and bring life to fiction, contrasting it with his own inability to act decisively in reality. This introspection highlights the idea of life as a performance, with individuals playing various roles and struggling with authenticity.

Another example is the play within the play in Act 2, Scene 2, often referred to as "The Mousetrap." Hamlet uses this play to test Claudius's guilt in the murder of King Hamlet. This meta-theatrical device highlights the idea of life as a performance, where characters take on roles and engage in acts of deception. This idea is central to the play's exploration of identity and the question of whether one can escape the roles they are expected to play.

In addition to his plays, Shakespeare also explored this idea in his sonnets. Sonnet 23,[6] for example, compares the poet's struggle to express his feelings to that of an actor struggling to deliver his lines on stage. The metaphor of the theater is used to convey the idea that the poet is trying to create an authentic performance of his emotions, just as an actor tries to create an authentic performance of their character:

As an unperfect actor on the stage,
Who with his fear is put besides his part,
Or some fierce thing replete with too much rage,

Whose strength's abundance weakens his own heart;

So I, for fear of trust, forget to say
The perfect ceremony of love's rite,
And in mine own love's strength seem to decay,
O'er-charg'd with burthen of mine own love's might.

O, let my books be then the eloquence
And dumb presagers of my speaking breast,
Who plead for love, and look for recompense,
More than that tongue that more hath more expressed.

O, learn to read what silent love hath writ:
To hear with eyes belongs to love's fine wit.

The idea that we are always performing is a concept that has been explored by various disciplines, including sociology, philosophy, and literature. One of the earliest and most influential thinkers on this topic is Erving Goffman, whose book *The Presentation of Self in Everyday Life* (1959) introduced the concept of "dramaturgy."[7] Goffman argued that social life is like a theater, where individuals perform different roles and put on a "front" to manage the impression they give to others. According to Goffman, these performances are not just limited to formal settings, such as job interviews or public speeches, but are present in everyday interactions as well.

According to Goffman, individuals engage in "impression management" by carefully selecting, rehearsing, and presenting themselves in a particular way to their audience, whether it be in a social, professional, or personal setting. Goffman argues that these performances are not only based on the individual's true identity but also shaped by social norms, roles, and expectations. In other words, individuals are always "performing" their identities, and these performances are key to shaping social interactions and relationships.

Building on Goffman's work, Judith Butler in her book *Gender Trouble* (1990) argued that gender is not an innate characteristic, but a performance that is repeated and reinforced through social norms and expectations. Butler's ideas have been influential in the fields of gender studies and queer theory, where scholars have explored the performative aspects of gender, sexuality, and identity.

In literature, other than in Shakespeare's work, the idea of performance has been explored in various ways. One notable example is Oscar Wilde's play *The Importance of Being Earnest* (1895),[8] which satirizes the idea of social performance and the hypocrisy of Victorian society. The play's characters constantly engage in performative acts, pretending to be someone they are not in order to fit in with social expectations.

Another example is Truman Capote's *In Cold Blood* (1966),[9] a true crime novel that blurs the lines between reality and performance. Capote's use of fictional techniques, such as dialogue and omniscient narration, creates a sense of dramatic tension and suggests that the events he is describing are themselves a kind of performance.

In philosophy, the idea of performance has been used to question the nature of reality itself. Jean Baudrillard, in his book *Simulacra and Simulation* (1981),[10] argues that in contemporary society, reality has been replaced by "simulacra" or simulations that are no longer based on any real referent. Baudrillard suggests that everything in our society is a performance, and that we have lost touch with any underlying reality.

The metaphor or leadership as performance

The metaphor of leadership as performance suggests that leadership is not just a set of fixed traits or behaviors, but rather a dynamic process that can be adapted and adjusted in different contexts. This metaphor has gained significant attention in the leadership literature in recent years, with scholars examining the ways in which leadership is enacted in organizations. One of the earliest references to this metaphor can be found in James MacGregor Burns' seminal work *Leadership* (1978),[11] where he suggests that leadership is acting, in that leaders must use their skills to communicate their vision to their followers. Burns argues that like an actor, a leader must play a role, taking on different personas to suit different situations, and that leadership is ultimately a performance.

Another influential author who has explored the leadership as performance metaphor is Gail Fairhurst. In her book *The Power of*

Framing: Creating the Language of Leadership (1995),[12] Fairhurst argues that leaders use language to frame their ideas, just as actors use language to frame a character. She suggests that the leader's use of language and communication is central to their role as an actor, shaping their followers' understanding of their vision.

More recently, scholars have used the metaphor of leadership as performance to explore the emotional intelligence required for effective leadership. In their book *Primal Leadership: Realizing the Power of Emotional Intelligence* (2002),[13] Daniel Goleman, Richard Boyatzis, and Annie McKee suggest that leaders must be able to display a range of emotions to connect with their followers, just as actors must be able to portray a range of emotions to connect with their audience. They argue that emotional intelligence is essential for leaders to be effective actors, creating a sense of trust and connection with their followers.

Mats Alvesson and Stefan Sveningsson (2003)[14] argue that leadership is a "dramaturgical phenomenon" in which leaders must carefully construct their identities and behaviors to suit the situation. For them, leadership is not just about being authentic, but rather about being able to perform different roles in different contexts.

One study by Min-Hsuan Lee and Kim Yang (2019)[15] argues that leadership self-presentation can be understood through the lens of acting, with leaders engaging in self-presentation strategies to influence their followers. They suggest that recognizing the performative aspect of leadership can help explain the impact of leaders' self-presentation on followers' work outcomes. In another study, Sudeshna Sengupta, Amit Jaiswal, and Prashant Kumar (2021)[16] explore the broader concept of leadership as a performance, suggesting that leadership is not just about enacting a role but is also about creating shared meaning and identity. They argue that understanding leadership as a performance can help to shed light on the complex role of leadership in shaping organizational culture and identity.

Overall, the metaphor of leadership as performance has proven to be a valuable way of thinking about leadership, emphasizing the importance of adaptation, context, and communication. By viewing leadership as a dynamic and flexible process, leaders can gain a deeper understanding of the complex challenges and opportunities involved in leading others.

The art of leadership

In this book, we conceptualize leadership as more than a role—it's an art form that requires mastery of five key skills: self-awareness, a strong presence, authenticity, clear communication, and emotional connection. Each of these skills is crucial for effective leadership; they complement each other and have an impact on both leaders and their followers. In Chapters 4 through 8, we explore how they can be developed through acting techniques.

By mastering these skills, a leader transcends the traditional authoritative role, embarking on a journey that impacts both themselves and their followers. This nuanced approach to leadership turns it into an art form, where the leader, just like a skilled performer, navigates the complexities of leading others in changing environments. This book aims to show how cultivating these skills through acting techniques can transform an ordinary leader into an extraordinary one, capable of making a lasting impact in their field.

There are many examples of leaders who are masters of the art of leadership. They demonstrate how the integration of self-awareness, presence, authenticity, clear communication, and emotional connection can lead to exceptional leadership. One such leader is Nelson Mandela, whose profound self-awareness and authentic presence played a key role in dismantling apartheid in South Africa. Mandela's ability to communicate clearly and connect emotionally with not just his supporters, but also his adversaries, showcases the power of these skills in creating transformative change.

Another example is Angela Merkel, the former chancellor of Germany. Known for her steady presence and pragmatic communication style, Merkel led Germany and Europe through numerous crises, demonstrating how effective leadership involves a balance of strength and empathy.

Let's delve into the case of Jacinda Ardern. Her journey as the former prime minister of New Zealand offers a unique perspective on how these skills play out in political leadership, especially during times of national crisis. Born on July 26, 1980, in Hamilton, New Zealand, Ardern's political career was marked by rapid growth. Joining the Labour Party at 17, she worked as a researcher before moving to London. Her return to New Zealand saw her rise to become a member of parliament in 2008, and later, the leader of the Labour Party in 2017. Ardern's leadership is recognized for her response to significant national crises, including the Christchurch mosque shootings and the COVID-19 pandemic. She resigned as prime minister in January 2023.[17]

Ardern connects with her followers at an emotional level, much like an actor connects with their audience. Her public appearances often show a deep understanding of the mood and needs of her audience. She adapts her communication style accordingly, just like a performer responding to the audience's reactions during a performance. Her speeches and public interactions are often marked by authenticity and emotional resonance, key elements in effective theatrical performance. This ability to "perform" in a manner that is both genuine and impactful is a significant aspect of her leadership style.

In addition, Ardern is very good at conveying empathy and understanding in her speeches, TV interviews, and appearances on social media. This was particularly noticeable following the Christchurch mosque shootings, where as part of her empathetic response, she chose to wear a hijab when meeting the Muslim community after the incident. This was a powerful gesture of solidarity and respect. Also, during the COVID-19 pandemic, Ardern's regular press briefings showcased her ability to empathize with those who were struggling with the virus. She was able to adapt her tone and message to the evolving situation, much like a performer adapts to the changing dynamics of a scene.

Ardern's authenticity is reminiscent of the most compelling stage performances, where the audience feels a deep, personal connection with the actor. We see her authenticity in her informal Facebook Live chats, where she interacts with the public in a casual, unscripted manner, reminiscent of a performer breaking the fourth wall to connect directly with the audience.

Ardern is also skilled at crafting and delivering a narrative, much like a storyteller, ensuring her message is not only heard but felt by her audience. In her election campaigns and policy announcements, she is able to craft compelling narratives that outline her vision for New Zealand, like a skillful actor setting the scene and guiding the audience through the plot.

Conclusion

Leadership can be seen as a performance, similar to a conductor leading an orchestra or an actor portraying a character. It requires a combination of skills, qualities, and actions performed in an intentional way to achieve a desired outcome. But the metaphor of leadership as a performance extends beyond mere analogy; it contains the essence of leadership. The performance aspect is not limited to the superficial act of "putting on a show." Instead, it is about the leader's ability to connect, inspire, and lead authentically.

In this chapter, we've explored leadership and performance through a diverse range of literature, from classical philosophy to contemporary leadership studies. Figures such as Plato, Shakespeare, James MacGregor Burns, and contemporary researchers like Mats Alvesson and Stefan Sveningsson provide insights into the metaphor of leadership as performance. Additionally, we've examined Erving Goffman's idea of the presentation of self, highlighting how individuals strategically manage impressions, just like actors do on a stage.

The metaphor of leadership as a performance also invites deeper reflections on the nature of leadership itself. It suggests that leadership is an art form that requires continuous refinement. This perspective encourages current and aspiring leaders to view their leadership as a life-long developmental process. By adopting this viewpoint, leaders can take control of their own leadership, hone it, and improve it. The metaphor encourages leaders to engage in self-reflection and to consider the impact of their "performance" on those they lead.

Reflective questions

- What are some similarities and differences between leadership and acting? How might understanding these similarities and differences help you become a more effective leader?
- How can Goffman's idea that as individuals, we are always "performing" our identities, help you understand and shape your role as a leader?
- Think about some of the roles that you play in your everyday life: parent, son, friend, co-worker, leader. Reflect on how

differently you behave depending on the role you're playing. Think about the adjustments that you make when you move from one role to the other. For example, notice the way your voice changes when you talk to your boss versus when you talk to your pet. Write or discuss with somebody your reflections.

•   What are some practical steps that you can take, as a leader, to incorporate acting techniques into your leadership practices so that you become more a effective leader?

•   Imagine that you have been appointed CEO of a Fortune 500 company. Close your eyes and visualize the way you look as the new CEO, what you're wearing, how you talk, what your office looks like. Picture yourself leading a meeting. Notice the way people look at you. Realize the impact that your words have on others. Once you have a clear picture, open your eyes and write or discuss with somebody how playing the CEO role is different from your regular role at work.

Notes

1 Duchen, J. (2011, July 31). Miracle maestro: Gustavo Dudamel brings music from Venezuela's slums to the Proms. *The Independent*. https://www.independent.co.uk/arts-entertainment/classical/features/miracle-maestro-gustavo-dudamel-brings-music-from-venezuela-s-slums-to-the-proms-2331731.html

2 Kosman, J. (2022, April 22). Review: Gustavo Dudamel mixes power and placidity with S.F. Symphony. *San Francisco Chronicle*. https://datebook.sfchronicle.com/music/review-gustavo-dudamel-mixes-power-and-placidity-with-sf-symphony

3 Schultz, H., & Yang, J. (2012). *Onward: How Starbucks Fought for Its Life Without Losing Its Soul*. New York, NY: Rodale Books.

4 Shakespeare, W. (1600). *As You Like It*. London, UK: Thomas Fisher.

5 Shakespeare, W. (1603). *Hamlet*. (T. Bevington, Ed.). Bantam Books.

6 Shakespeare, W. (1609). Sonnet 23 [Poem]. In P. H. Mussen (Ed.), *The Complete Sonnets and Poems* (pp. 59). Oxford University Press. (Original work published 1609.)

7 Goffman, E. (1959). *The Presentation of Self in Everyday Life*. Garden City, NY: Doubleday.

8 Wilde, O. (1895). *The Importance of Being Earnest*. London, UK: Samuel French Ltd.

9 Capote, T. (1966). *In Cold Blood*. New York, NY: Random House.

10 Baudrillard, J. (1981). *Simulacra and Simulation*. University of Michigan Press.

11 Burns, J. M. (1978). *Leadership*. Harper & Row

12 Fairhurst, G. T. (1995). *The Power of Framing: Creating the Language of Leadership*. Jossey-Bass.

13 Goleman, D., Boyatzis, R. E., & McKee, A. (2002). *Primal Leadership: Realizing the Power of Emotional Intelligence*. Harvard Business Review Press.

14 Alvesson, M., & Sveningsson, S. (2003). The great disappearing act: Difficulties in doing "leadership". The Leadership Quarterly, 14(3), 359–381.

15 Lee, M., & Yang, K. (2019). The leader as actor: How leaders' self-presentation influences followers' work outcomes. Academy of Management Review, 44(2), 386–409.

16 Sengupta, S., Jaiswal, A., & Kumar, P. (2021). Acting it out: Exploring leadership as a performance. Journal of Business Research, 130, 102–113.

17 Britannica. (n.d.). Jacinda Ardern | Biography, Facts, & Partner. Retrieved from https://www.britannica.com/biography/Jacinda-Ardern.

2   Fundamentals of acting

Malaysian actress Michelle Yeoh, who won an Oscar for her role in *Everything Everywhere All at Once*, is known for her extraordinary ability to immerse herself in her characters. Her capacity to understand her character's history and motivations has been praised by critics and audiences alike. In an interview with *Time Magazine* in 2022, Yeoh said: "Every time I take on a role, I have to give her history. I have to know where she's coming from."[1]

In the movie *Everything Everywhere All at Once*, Yeoh portrays a humble accountant turned multiverse-hopping hero. We see her navigating multiple realities with rich emotional depth. What sets Yeoh's performance apart is her character's ability to interact with different versions of herself across multiple universes, displaying ease and humor even in the face of challenging circumstances. Through her character's journey, Yeoh shows the importance of inspiring, adapting, and leading in the face of adversity.

This chapter explores the fundamentals of acting, providing a foundation for the rest of the book. It begins by giving a brief overview of the evolution of acting and theater, highlighting key historical periods and styles. Then, it focuses on method acting, the most widely used technique in contemporary Western theater. The method, as it is commonly known, was developed by the Russian actor and director Konstantin Stanislavski. It encourages actors to draw on their personal experiences and memories to bring authenticity and realism to their performance. Finally, the chapter explores the four acting approaches that are at the core of the exercises used in this book for developing leadership skills: Uta Hagen's Technique, Stella Adler's Technique, the Meisner Technique, and the Viola Spolin's Method.

DOI: 10.4324/9781003349815-3

A brief history of acting and theater

Throughout the world, the art of acting and theater has a rich and diverse history that spans cultures and regions. In ancient Greece, theater was an important part of society, with performances featuring actors in masks portraying characters in tragedies and comedies. These plays were performed in open-air amphitheaters and were attended by thousands of people. The Greeks developed a highly stylized form of theater, emphasizing exaggerated gestures and vocal inflections to convey emotion and meaning to the audience. Tragedies often dealt with serious subjects like family conflict, political turmoil, and the nature of the gods, while comedies were more lighthearted, often poking fun at societal norms and figures of authority. Notable Greek playwrights include Aeschylus, Sophocles, and Euripides, who wrote some of the most enduring works of Western literature.[2]

During the Roman Empire, theater became an even more prominent part of society, with a variety of topics and genres being explored. Performances took place in grand theaters and arenas, and were heavily influenced by Greek theater. However, the Romans developed their own unique style and conventions. Elaborate costumes, music, and dance were used to enhance the performances, which were not only used to entertain, but also to educate and communicate important messages. In addition to comedy and tragedy, other genres like mime, Atellan Farce, and satire were also popular. The topics of the plays ranged from mythology and history to daily life and social commentary. Theater was a way to celebrate important events such as victories in battle, and was often used as a tool of propaganda by the ruling elite.[3]

In India, Sanskrit drama is regarded as the earliest theatrical tradition, dating back to the 2nd century BCE. This form of drama was typically performed by traveling troupes and was known for its elaborate sets, costumes, and incorporation of music and dance. Sanskrit drama explored a variety of themes, including morality, religion, and politics, and followed a five-act structure with highly stylized acting, emphasizing hand gestures, facial expressions, and body movements. Over time, Sanskrit drama evolved into other forms of Indian theater, such as the folk theater jatra in Bengal and the highly stylized dance-drama kathakali in Kerala, but it remains a significant part of India's cultural heritage and continues to inspire contemporary theatre.[4]

In China, theatre has a rich history dating back over two thousand years, with a diverse range of forms including opera, puppetry, and shadow play. One of the most famous forms is Beijing Opera, which features singing, dancing, acrobatics, and martial arts, and explores themes such as loyalty, justice, and revenge. The acting style in Chinese theatre is highly physical, emphasizing gestures, facial expressions, and body movements, and often uses symbolism and metaphor to convey deeper meanings. Beijing opera, for example, emphasizes the beauty of movement, voice, and facial expression to convey the emotions and storylines of the characters.[5]

In Japan, traditional theater has a rich history that includes noh, kabuki, and bunraku. Noh theater originated in the 14th century and is known for its use of masks, stylized movement, and haunting music. It often explores themes related to Buddhism and Japanese mythology. Kabuki, on the other hand, emerged in the 17th century and features elaborate makeup and costumes, as well as exaggerated gestures and vocal inflections. Kabuki is known for its use of male actors who portray female roles, known as onnagata. Bunraku is a form of puppet theater that developed in the 17th century and features intricate puppets manipulated by puppeteers who remain visible on stage. Bunraku often explores themes related to Japanese history and folklore.[6]

Following the fall of the Roman Empire, theater and acting largely disappeared from European culture until the medieval period, when drama once again became an important part of religious festivals and ceremonies. Mystery plays, which dramatized biblical stories and themes, were performed by traveling actors in town squares and other public spaces. These performances were often highly stylized and featured exaggerated gestures and vocal inflections to convey meaning to the audience.[7]

During the Renaissance period, theater and acting underwent a significant transformation throughout Europe. With the construction of purpose-built theaters and the rise of professional actors, a new style of performance emerged that captivated audiences. The works of William Shakespeare, Molière, and Lope de Vega were celebrated throughout Europe, each with their unique acting styles. Shakespeare's plays were known for their poetic and dramatic delivery, with actors using elaborate gestures and vocal inflections to convey the meaning of the text. Molière also employed a highly stylized and theatrical acting style characterized by exaggerated gestures and vocal inflections. This style was in keeping with the conventions of French neoclassical theater, which emphasized formal structure, decorum, and heightened language. Lope de Vega's plays often required actors to portray multiple roles, which demanded versatility and skill. Meanwhile, the emergence of commedia dell'arte in Italy introduced a highly improvisational acting style that featured exaggerated gestures and physical comedy.[8]

During the 18th and 19th centuries, theater and acting underwent further transformations, marked by the rise of realism and naturalism. The aim of these styles was to create performances that were more believable and truer to life. This period also saw the emergence of new forms of theater such as melodrama, which focused on exaggerated emotions and dramatic spectacle. Melodramas were often characterized by a clear division between good and evil, with the hero and heroine pitted against the villain in a series of suspenseful scenes. Another popular form of theater during this period was the well-made play, which featured intricate plots, surprise twists, and tightly constructed narratives.[9]

Acting techniques also evolved during this period, with actors increasingly focused on portraying characters in a realistic and believable way. The Stanislavski system, also known as the method, developed by the Russian actor and director Konstantin Stanislavski, became popular in the early 20th century and emphasized the use of emotional memory, physical actions, and detailed character analysis. This system revolutionized acting by introducing a more naturalistic and psychological approach, encouraging actors to create characters with depth and nuance. The following section deals with the principles of method acting, which is today the most widely known acting approach in the Western world.

The Method

The Method, also known as method acting or the Stanislavski Method, is a technique used by actors to create a deep emotional connection between themselves and the characters they are portraying.[10] The technique was developed by Russian actor and director Konstantin Stanislavski in the early 20th century, and it revolutionized the way actors approached their craft.

At the heart of the Method is the belief that actors must draw on their own experiences and emotions to create authentic and believable performances. In order to do this, actors are encouraged to engage in a process of emotional recall, in which they draw on their own memories and experiences to recreate the emotional state of their characters. Stanislavski emphasized that the actor's goal is to live truthfully under the imaginary circumstances of the play.

The Method is characterized by a series of exercises and techniques designed to help actors achieve this emotional connection. One of the most well-known exercises is the "Magic If," in which actors ask themselves what they would do if they were in the same situation as their characters. This exercise helps actors to identify with their characters on a deep level and to create performances that are both authentic and emotionally resonant.

Another key element of the Method is the use of sensory and physical exercises to help actors develop a sense of their character's physical and emotional presence. Actors might, for example, engage in exercises designed to help them develop a sense of their character's posture, movement, and physical gestures. These exercises help actors to create performances that are grounded in the physical reality of the character, and that feel authentic and true to life.

The Method was introduced to the United States in the 1930s by Lee Strasberg, a former student of Stanislavski's. Strasberg developed his own version of the Method, which became known as the "Method of Physical Actions." This version of the Method placed an even greater emphasis on physical and sensory exercises, and on the development of a deep emotional connection between the actor and the character.

In the years since its introduction, the Method has become one of the most widely used acting techniques in the Western world. It has been embraced by actors ranging from Marlon Brando to Meryl Streep, and has been used in countless productions on stage and screen.

However, the Method is not without its critics. Some have argued that the technique places too much emphasis on emotional intensity, and that it can lead to actors becoming so deeply immersed in their characters that they lose touch with reality. Others have argued that the Method is too inward-focused, and that it can lead actors to neglect the physical and external aspects of their performances.

Despite these criticisms, the Method remains an important and influential technique in the world of acting. Its emphasis on emotional authenticity and connection has helped countless actors to create performances that are both moving and memorable, and its impact on the world of theater and film cannot be overstated.

Four key acting approaches

In this section, we explore the four acting approaches behind the leadership development exercises in the book: Uta Hagen's Technique, Stella Adler's Technique, the Meisner Technique, and Viola Spolin's Method. They were chosen because they are all commonly used in the world of acting, but they can also be valuable tools for leaders looking to improve their leadership skills. Each of these techniques has its own unique strengths and focuses, but they all share a common goal of helping actors connect more deeply with themselves, with their characters and with others.

Uta Hagen's Technique

Uta Hagen was a Broadway actor and acting teacher born in Germany in 1919 but raised in the United States. She developed an acting technique[11] based on the Method, and emphasized the importance of rigorous observation of daily life. Hagen's technique involved five key elements: substitution, transference, specificity, authenticity, and preparation. Her substitution technique focused on the actor convincingly putting themselves in the circumstances of the performance, rather than importing their own life's defining moments into their work. Transference involved finding the actor's relationship to the character based on their own experience and perspective, while specificity required rehearsing with the specific props that would be used in the final performance. Authenticity emphasized utilizing props, costumes, or architectural features to motivate authentic action, while preparation involved observing human behavior and rehearsing to develop authentic behavior and perform a role fluently. Hagen's technique is a middle ground between internal work (targeting feelings, motivations, inner thoughts) and external work (targeting physicality, posture, voice).

Hagen's technique was influenced by her own experience as a Broadway actor, where she played some of the most iconic roles during the golden age of American theater. Her best-known roles include the title role in *Saint Joan*, Blanche DuBois in *A Streetcar Named Desire*, Desdemona in *Othello*, and Martha in the premiere of *Who's Afraid of Virginia Woolf?* She also received several Tony Awards for her acting and a National Medal of Honor for the Arts for her contributions to American theater.

In 1947, Hagen began teaching at her husband's acting studio, the Herbert Berghof Studio (HB Studio), which still teaches her techniques today. Her teaching style was marked by a focus on the actor's process, rather than the finished product. Hagen encouraged actors to avoid over-intellectualizing their processes and instead to root themselves in rigorous observation of daily life. She believed that this would help actors develop a deeper emotional connection to the characters they portrayed and create more authentic and compelling performances.

Hagen's technique has had a significant impact on the world of acting, and her legacy is still felt today. Her approach to teaching acting is respected for its focus on the actor's process and its emphasis on rigorous observation of daily life. Many actors continue to use her techniques to this day, and her contributions to the world of theater continue to be celebrated. In the 1990s, I was fortunate to train as an actor for many years at the HB Studio in New York, where I learned most of what I know about acting and theater. Many of the leadership development exercises in the book are based on Hagen's teachings.

Stella Adler's Technique

Stella Adler was a legendary figure in the world of American theater, known not only for her accomplished acting career but also for her innovative approach to teaching acting. Born in New York City in 1901, Adler came from a family of prominent Yiddish theater performers and was introduced to the world of acting at an early age. She honed her craft through years of training and experience, becoming a celebrated actor in her own right.

Adler's interest in acting technique led her to study with the likes of Konstantin Stanislavski and other prominent theater practitioners. In the 1930s, she joined the Group Theatre, a groundbreaking ensemble that aimed to bring a more realistic style of acting to the American stage. However, Adler grew frustrated with the approach of Lee Strasberg, another member of the Group who emphasized the use of affective memory, or personal recall of past experiences, as a means of accessing emotions. Adler believed this technique was limiting and potentially harmful, particularly for younger actors. Seeking clarification on Stanislavski's original teachings, Adler traveled to Paris to meet with the master himself. There, she learned that Stanislavski had moved away from affective memory and was advocating for a more holistic approach to acting that focused on imagination, physicality, and sensory awareness. With this knowledge, Adler returned to the United States and developed her own approach to teaching acting, which emphasized the importance of emotional connection, imagination, and sensory work. She became one of the most respected and influential acting teachers of the 20th century, with many of her students going on to become successful actors in their own right.

The Stella Adler technique[12] focuses on an actor's imagination and ability to immerse themselves in a character's world, expanding their understanding of the world to create compelling performances. The technique stresses discipline, text analysis, and action. Adler believed in maintaining discipline to improve performance, analyzing the text for key elements that dictate the character's nature and circumstances, and focusing on action as something one character does to another to elicit a specific response. Overall, the Adler technique is a powerful tool for actors seeking to develop a deep emotional connection to the characters they portray and create authentic and compelling performances. The technique can be equally useful for leaders as it emphasizes the importance of imagination and empathy, allowing leaders to create a clear vision and connect with their followers on a deeper emotional level.

The Meisner Technique

Sanford Meisner was an actor and acting teacher born in New York in 1905. He trained with the Theatre Guild before becoming a founding member of The Group Theatre. Meisner's technique emphasizes the importance of an actor's connection to their scene partner, which he thought contributed to creating a sense

of tension and authenticity on stage. His approach is characterized by a series of exercises designed to help actors fully immerse
themselves in the moment and deliver compelling performances.

The Meisner Technique[13] consists of three main tenets:
emotional preparation, repetition, and improvisation. Meisner
believed that emotional preparation involves doing whatever is
necessary to enter a scene "emotionally alive." He instructed
actors to use personal experiences or imagined circumstances
to put themselves in their character's emotional state. Meisner
also used repetition exercises to develop his students' skills of
observation and instinct, teaching that these authentic instincts
capture realistic human behavior. Finally, Meisner believed in
the power of improvisation and flexibility in a performance.
According to him, actors should not make any choices on stage
until something provokes them, thereby justifying their behavior.

One of the key concepts in the Meisner Technique is that of the
"as if" scenario, where an actor approaches a scene as if it were
really happening to them. This element is also present in Uta Hagen's
method. The "as if," or "Magic If" as it is also known, allows actors
to fully engage emotionally with the scene and the other actors, creating a more authentic performance. Meisner also believed that a
strong foundation in the basics of acting, such as voice and movement, was essential to building a successful career as an actor.

The Meisner Technique involves exercises that help actors
connect with their scene partners and respond truthfully in the
moment. Some of these exercises will be applied in this book to
help leaders develop better communication skills, build stronger
relationships with their teams, and foster a more engaging work
environment. Additionally, the Meisner Technique's focus on
improvisation is often used in the exercises of the book to promote creative problem-solving and help leaders think on their
feet. The next approach, based on Viola Spolin's teachings, has
improvisation at the heart of its method.

The Viola Spolin Method

Viola Spolin was a theater arts innovator who was born in
Chicago in 1906. She learned about the benefits of group play
among children while studying under a sociologist at a local settle-
ment house, which later influenced her pioneering improvisation

techniques onstage. In 1946, Spolin founded the Young Actors Company, where she developed her Theater Games. She continued to refine her techniques in Chicago with the Compass Players and Second City Company. She passed on her teachings to her protégés who continued to spread her techniques in newly spawned improv schools and acting companies.

Until her death in 1994, Spolin directed children's theater, led workshops for television casts, and founded the Spolin Theater Game Center where professional coaches were trained to teach her techniques. Spolin's Theater Games System, also known as the Spolin Technique,[14] has become a widely recognized approach in improvisation, stagecraft, and comedy, popularizing the improv comedy movement. Her exercises are designed to ground actors in the present moment, allowing them to create action and character development with their scene partners and audience on the fly, while encouraging freedom of expression and discouraging self-consciousness.

According to Spolin, one of the main purposes of her techniques is to help actors get out of their heads and into their bodies, by developing a sense of awareness of the present moment and their surroundings. Her games and exercises are designed to foster spontaneity and improvisation, and to create a sense of community among actors.

Spolin's exercises have been influential not just in theater, but also in areas such as education, therapy, and business. Leaders can benefit a great deal from Spolin's improvisation exercises considering how crucial it is for leaders to think on their feet, make quick decisions, and adapt to changing situations. In addition, leaders can benefit from spontaneous thinking, active listening, and effective communication, which are also skills that are developed through improvisation. By encouraging participants to let go of their inhibitions and tap into their natural creativity, improvisation gives leaders the opportunity to approach problems from new and unexpected angles, foster a more positive and productive work environment, and build stronger relationships.

Conclusion

This chapter explored various periods and styles of acting, while making relevant connections with the field of leadership. It focused on Stanislavski's Method, highlighting the significance of authenticity within this approach. The chapter also introduced four key acting approaches: Uta Hagen's Technique, Stella Adler's Technique, the Meisner Technique, and Viola Spolin's Method. These approaches serve as foundational elements for the leadership development exercises in this book. Their focus on understanding the action, using the imagination, making connections with others, and embracing improvisation provides valuable insights for nurturing effective leadership skills.

Reflective questions

- How has the history of acting and theater influenced the development of modern acting techniques, and in what ways can these techniques be applied to the way you lead others?
- How might Konstantin Stanislavski's Method, with its emphasis on authenticity and emotional recall, be beneficial for you as a leader?
- Review the main elements of Uta Hagen's Technique. In what ways could you apply these elements to the development of your leadership skills?
- Review the main elements of Stella Adler's Technique. In what ways could you apply these elements to the development of your leadership skills?
- Review the main elements of the Meisner Technique. In what ways could you apply these elements to the development of your leadership skills?
- Review the main elements of Viola Spolin's Method. In what ways could you apply these elements to the development of your leadership skills?

Notes

1 Lang, C. (2022, April 5). Michelle Yeoh knows the secret to feeling limitless. Time. Retrieved from https://time.com/6163777/michelle -yeoh-everything-everywhere-all-at-once-interview/
2 Flickinger, R. C. (1922). *The Greek Theatre and Its Drama*. University of Chicago Press.
3 Wiles, D. (2004). *The Masks of Menander: Sign and Meaning in Greek and Roman Performance*. Cambridge University Press.

4 Lal, A. (2011). *The Oxford Handbook of Indian Theatre*. Oxford University Press.
5 Mackerras, C. (1983). *Chinese Theater: From Its Origins to the Present Day*. University of Hawaii Press.
6 Banham, M. (Ed.). (1995). *The Cambridge Guide to Theatre*. Cambridge University Press.
7 Harris, J. W. (1992). *Medieval Theatre in Context: An Introduction*. Routledge.
8 Vince, R. W. (1984). *Renaissance Theatre: A Historiographical Handbook*. ABC-CLIO LLC.
9 Hosein, A. (Ed.). (2016). *The History of Theater*. Britannica Educational Publishing.
10 Stanislavski, K. (1936). *An Actor Prepares*. Methuen Drama.
11 Ates, A. (2022, June 30). The definitive guide to Uta Hagen's acting technique. *Backstage*. https://www.backstage.com/magazine/article/the-definitive-guide-to-uta-hagens-acting-technique-68922/
12 Ates, A. (2021, March 26). The definitive guide to Stella Adler's acting technique. *Backstage*. https://www.backstage.com/magazine/article/the-definitive-guide-to-the-stella-adler-acting-technique-66369/
13 Ates, A. (2022, March 14). Meisner Technique: An actor's guide. *Backstage*. https://www.backstage.com/magazine/article/the-definitive-guide-to-the-meisner-technique-67712/
14 Backstage Staff. (2022, March 8). What is the Viola Spolin Method? *Backstage*. https://www.backstage.com/magazine/article/what-is-viola-spolin-technique-theater-games-74829/

3 Fundamentals of leadership

One of the best examples of how acting can impact leadership skills is Ronald Reagan's extraordinary ability to inspire. The former Hollywood star, who became the 40th president of the United States, believed a leader's role is to inspire and empower others rather than focusing solely on personal achievements. In an interview on CBS in 1975, Reagan said "The greatest leader is not necessarily the one who does the greatest things. He is the one who gets the people to do the greatest things."[1] His view underscores the idea that effective leadership is about inspiring and enabling followers to reach their highest potential.

It is clear that Reagan's experience as an actor significantly contributed to his effectiveness as a leader. His acting skills honed his ability to communicate persuasively, a key trait for any successful leader. He was known for being a wonderful storyteller, able to connect with the public and convey his political messages effectively. Reagan's exceptional communication skill earned him the nickname "The Great Communicator." His presence, honed through years of acting, also played a role in his ability to motivate people, an essential quality in leadership. This crossover of skills from acting to leadership is at the heart of this book.

This chapter covers the four most common conceptualizations of leadership, including leadership as a set of traits, behaviors, process, and relationship. Other conceptualizations of leadership such as situational leadership, transformational leadership, servant leadership, and authentic leadership are also discussed. By understanding these theories, readers will be able to identify the core qualities and skills required of effective leaders. Overall, this

DOI: 10.4324/9781003349815-4

chapter aims to provide a theoretical foundation for the rest of the book.

Leadership theories

The study of leadership can be traced back to ancient China approximately 2,500 years ago. *The Art of War*,[2] often credited to the Chinese philosopher and general Sun Tzu, is one of the most famous ancient texts on leadership. In a conversational format, the book provides a set of key strategic elements and tactics intended for military leaders. Ironically, one of the most significant lessons of *The Art of War* is that the real skill of a leader lies in the ability to avoid unnecessary conflict:

> In the practical art of war, the best thing of all is to take the enemy's country whole and intact; to shatter and destroy it is not so good. So, too, it is better to recapture an army entire than to destroy it, to capture a regiment, a detachment or a company entire than to destroy them (p. 46).

Just as the fundamentals of acting are built on a foundation of techniques and principles that have been developed over time, the study of leadership is rooted in a rich history of theory and practice. From the earliest forms of leadership in ancient civilizations to the modern-day workplace, leadership theories have emerged to help us better understand what makes a great leader and how we can develop the skills and abilities necessary to lead effectively.

Throughout history, various leadership theories have appeared in response to different societal and cultural contexts, ranging from authoritarian and hierarchical leadership in ancient empires to more democratic and participative leadership in modern democracies. These theories have been shaped by historical events, such as wars, revolutions, and social movements, that have highlighted the importance of strong and effective leadership in times of crisis and change.

This section explores some of the most influential leadership theories that have emerged over the years in the 20th and 21st centuries, from trait theory which focuses on the individual characteristics of effective leaders, to behavioral theory which emphasizes observable behaviors that distinguish successful leaders from unsuccessful ones, to contingency theory which stresses the importance of adapting leadership style to fit the situation. We will also examine more recent theories, such as transformational leadership, followership, servant leadership, and authentic leadership. These theories place a greater emphasis on the emotional and ethical dimensions of leadership, and look at how these factors can impact organizational performance. By understanding the strengths and weaknesses of these various theories, and how they have been influenced by historical events and social contexts, we can gain a more comprehensive understanding of what it takes to be an effective leader.

Trait theory

The trait theory of leadership suggests that certain personal characteristics, such as intelligence, confidence, and sociability, are inherently linked to effective leadership. This theory emerged in the early 20th century, at a time when there was growing interest in identifying the key qualities that distinguish great leaders from their followers.

Ralph Stogdill's influential 1948 paper on the trait approach to leadership identified several core traits that were associated with effective leadership, including intelligence, dominance, self-confidence, and social adaptability. Stogdill also noted that the significance of these traits could vary depending on the context in which leadership was being exercised, and that situational factors could play an important role in determining which traits were most important.[3]

Victor Vroom and Philip Yetton's 1973 book, *Leadership and Decision Making*, built on the work of Stogdill and others by examining how specific traits related to decision-making processes in organizations. They suggested that effective leaders possessed certain cognitive abilities, such as problem-solving skills and the ability to think critically and creatively, as well as personality traits such as extraversion and emotional stability.[4]

Despite its historical significance, the trait theory of leadership has been criticized for oversimplifying the complex nature of leadership, and for failing to account for situational and contextual factors that can shape leadership effectiveness. In addition, the theory exhibits a male bias as evidenced by the fact that the majority of the research on leadership traits was conducted on male leaders. The traits that were identified as being important for effective leadership were often based on male gender stereotypes. This led to a perception that leadership was a male-dominated domain, and that women were less suited to leadership roles. More recent research has challenged these assumptions and highlighted the importance of gender diversity in leadership. Studies have shown that traits traditionally associated with femininity, such as empathy and compassion, are also valuable leadership qualities. As a result, contemporary leadership theories and models tend to be more inclusive and emphasize the importance of diversity and inclusion in leadership.

Behavioral theory

The behavioral theory of leadership emerged in the 1950s, at a time when scholars were beginning to question the validity of the trait theory of leadership. This new theory proposed that the most effective leaders were not simply born with certain inherent traits, but rather that their leadership skills were developed through their behavior and actions.

Philip Selznick's 1957 book *Leadership in Administration: A Sociological Interpretation* was one of the earliest works to emphasize the importance of behavior in leadership. Selznick argued that leaders must be attuned to the needs and goals of their followers, and must work to create a sense of shared purpose and common values within their organization. He also stressed the importance of ethical leadership and the need for leaders to act with integrity and fairness.[5]

Frederick Herzberg, Bernard Mausner, and Barbara Bloch Snyderman's 1959 book *The Motivation to Work* further developed the behavioral theory of leadership by examining the relationship between job satisfaction and job performance. They found that employees who were more satisfied with their jobs tended to perform better and were more likely to be motivated to achieve organizational goals. This led to the development of the two-factor theory of motivation, which posited that there were certain factors (such as pay and job security) that were necessary for job satisfaction, but did not necessarily lead to motivation, and other factors (such as recognition and opportunities for advancement) that were key drivers of motivation and job performance.[6]

One of the main criticisms of the behavioral theory of leadership is that it oversimplifies the complex nature of leadership by reducing it to a set of observable behaviors. Critics argue that effective leadership involves much more than just specific behaviors, and that situational and contextual factors play a significant role in determining leadership effectiveness. Another criticism is that it can be difficult to identify which specific behaviors are most important for effective leadership. Different situations may require different behaviors, and what works for one leader in one situation may not work for another leader in a different situation. This has led to the development of contingency theories of leadership, which emphasize the importance of adapting leadership style to fit the situation.

Contingency theory

The contingency theory of leadership emerged in the 1960s as a response to the limitations of earlier trait and behavioral theories of leadership. The basic premise of this theory is that there is no one "best" style of leadership that is effective in all situations; instead, the most effective leadership style depends on the specific circumstances at hand.

Fred Fiedler's 1964 article "A Contingency Model of Leadership Effectiveness" was one of the earliest and most influential works on contingency theory. Fiedler proposed that the effectiveness of a leader was contingent on three key factors: the leader's style, the favorability of the situation, and the leader's control over the situation. He argued that the most effective leaders were those whose leadership style matched the situational demands they faced.[7]

Robert House's 1971 book *Path-Goal Theory of Leadership* further developed the contingency theory by proposing that effective leaders must be able to adapt their leadership style to the needs of their followers and the demands of the situation. House argued that effective leaders provide their followers with a clear path to achieving their goals, and that the leader's role is to remove any obstacles that stand in the way of their followers' success.[8]

One of the main criticisms of the contingency theory of leadership is that it can be difficult to apply in practice, since it requires leaders to have a deep understanding of the specific situations that they are facing in order to select the most effective leadership style. Critics argue that this level of situational awareness can be difficult to achieve, and that some leaders may struggle to adapt their leadership style to fit the demands of different situations. Another criticism of the contingency theory is that it can be too simplistic in its assumptions about leadership effectiveness. Critics argue that effective leadership involves more than just adapting to situational demands, and that individual characteristics and traits may also play a significant role in determining leadership effectiveness.

Despite these criticisms, the contingency theory of leadership remains an important foundation for understanding the role of context and situational factors in determining leadership effectiveness, and has influenced many subsequent theories and models of leadership.

Servant leadership

Servant leadership theory emerged in the 1970s with the publication of Robert Greenleaf's essay *The Servant as Leader* in 1970.[9] Greenleaf proposed a new approach to leadership that emphasized the leader's role in serving others; he argued that the primary goal of a servant leader is to serve the needs of others. Servant leadership theory has since evolved to emphasize traits such as empathy, listening, and persuasion in effective servant leadership.[10]

While servant leadership has gained popularity and attention in recent years, it has also faced criticism from some researchers. One criticism is that servant leadership can be too focused on the needs of others, potentially neglecting the leader's own needs and priorities.[11] Another critique is that servant leadership can be difficult to implement in organizations that place a strong emphasis on power and authority.[12]

Despite criticism that it may neglect the leader's own needs and be challenging to implement in certain contexts, servant leadership continues to be influential in the field of leadership studies. Servant leadership emphasizes community, empathy, and collaboration, and can be observed in organizations that prior-itize employee well-being and community service. Leaders who embody servant leadership prioritize listening, empathy, and collaboration, and encourage personal and professional growth among their followers.

Transformational leadership

Transformational leadership as a theory emerged in the late 1970s and early 1980s. The concept was first introduced by James MacGregor Burns in his book *Leadership* in 1978,[13] where he contrasted transformational leadership with transactional leadership. Burns argued that transformational leaders inspire and motivate followers to achieve beyond their own self-interests, while transactional leaders focus on maintaining the status quo and providing rewards and punishments based on performance. Transformational leaders achieve this by creating a vision for the future, communicating that vision to others, and empowering fol-lowers to achieve that vision.

According to Burns, transformational leadership involves four key components: idealized influence, inspirational motiva-tion, intellectual stimulation, and individualized consideration. Idealized influence refers to the leader's ability to serve as a role model for their followers, gaining their trust and respect. Inspirational motivation involves the leader communicating a vision and inspiring followers to work towards that vision. Intellectual stimulation involves the leader encouraging creativity and innovation among followers, challenging them to think criti-cally and consider new perspectives. Individualized consideration involves the leader providing support and encouragement to indi-vidual followers, recognizing their unique needs and abilities.

Bass expanded on Burns' work and identified three addi-tional components of transformational leadership: charisma, stimulation of followers' emotions, and providing intellectual stimulation.[14] Charisma refers to the leader's ability to inspire and motivate followers through their personality and presence. Stimulation of followers' emotions involves the leader creating a sense of excitement and passion among followers for achieving the vision. Providing intellectual stimulation involves the leader challenging followers to think critically and creatively, promoting innovation and problem-solving.

Overall, transformational leadership theory suggests that leaders can have a significant impact on their followers' performance and growth by inspiring them to work towards a shared vision and empowering them to achieve that vision through individualized support and encouragement. However, transformational leadership theory has also received criticism from some researchers. One critique is that it can create a dependency on the leader, leading to a lack of accountability among followers.[15] Another criticism is that it can be too focused on the leader's charisma and personality, potentially leading to conflicts and resistance among followers if their needs and goals are not being addressed.[16] Additionally, some researchers have noted the lack of empirical evidence for the effectiveness of transformational leadership in certain contexts.[17] Despite these criticisms, transformational leadership remains a popular and influential theory in the field of leadership studies, and its impact on organizational performance and growth continues to be an area of research and study.

Followership theory

Followership theory emerged as a distinct field of study in the 1990s, although the concept of followership has been discussed in leadership literature for many decades. Robert Kelley's book *The Power of Followership* published in 1992 is often credited with popularizing the concept of followership and bringing attention to the importance of followers in the leadership process.[18] Followership theory emphasizes the important role that followers play in effective leadership. According to Kelley, followers are active participants in the leadership process, and they contribute to the success of their leaders and organizations through their own behavior, attitudes, and values. The theory proposes that followership can be developed and cultivated, and that effective followers are those who are able to engage in critical thinking, take initiative, and support their leaders.

One of the key strengths of followership theory is its focus on the role of followers in the leadership process. This perspective challenges the traditional view of leadership as a one-way relationship between the leader and followers and emphasizes the importance of followers in the success of organizations. As Uhl-Bien et al.[19] note, this can have important implications for leadership development and training as it highlights the need to develop followership skills alongside leadership skills.

Critics of followership theory, however, have argued that it places too much emphasis on the role of followers and not enough on the role of the leader.[20] They argue that while followership is an important component of effective leadership, it should not be viewed as a substitute for leadership. Another criticism is that followership theory can potentially lead to a lack of accountability among followers, as they may rely too heavily on their leaders for guidance and direction.[21]

Examples of followership theory in action can be seen in organizations that promote a culture of collaboration and shared decision-making. In these organizations, followers are encouraged to take an active role in the leadership process, and their contributions are valued and respected. By empowering followers to take ownership of their work and contribute to the success of the organization, leaders can create a culture of engagement and accountability that supports the goals of the organization.[22]

Authentic leadership theory

Authentic leadership theory emerged in the early 2000s. The theory proposes that effective leadership is based on a leader's ability to display genuine and transparent behavior, while encouraging others to do the same. Avolio and Gardner,[23] who created one of the most influential models on authentic leadership, emphasize the importance of four factors in authentic leadership: self-awareness, internalized moral perspective, balanced processing, and relational transparency.

Self-awareness involves being conscious of one's own thoughts, feelings, and behaviors, as well as how these impact others. Authentic leaders are self-reflective and seek feedback from others to gain a better understanding of themselves and their impact on others. Internalized moral perspective refers to the values and ethical principles that guide an individual's decision-making. Authentic leaders have a strong sense of ethics and are committed to acting in accordance with their values. Balanced processing involves the ability to consider multiple perspectives and gather diverse opinions before making a decision. Authentic leaders encourage open communication and actively seek out differing perspectives to inform their decision-making. Relational transparency involves being open and honest in communication with others, and building trusting relationships with followers. Authentic leaders prioritize open and honest communication, and are willing to share their personal experiences and emotions with others.

While the concept of authenticity has been criticized for being difficult to define and measure, Avolio and Gardner's model provides a framework for understanding the components of authentic leadership. Leaders who display these qualities of authentic leadership are more likely to inspire their followers to be more engaged and committed to their work.[24]

Conclusion

This chapter explored various leadership theories, each offering unique perspectives on what it means to lead. By recognizing the strengths and weaknesses of each theory and their historical and cultural contexts, leaders can cultivate the qualities and skills required for successful leadership. As the field of leadership continues to evolve, embracing diverse perspectives becomes essential for leaders to thrive in today's dynamic and complex world.

Reflective questions

- Which leadership theory (e.g., trait, behavioral, contingency, transformational, followership, servant, or authentic leadership) resonates with you the most, and why? Can you think of any real-world leaders who exemplify this theory?
- Think about the differences and similarities between trait theory and behavioral theory of leadership. How might understanding these theories help you become a more effective leader ?
- Imagine a very successful company which has been growing year after year. You are part of a team of consultants who study and research leadership. Write three specific leadership-related elements that your team is likely to discuss when

explaining the success of the company in each of the following cases:

- Your team specializes in leadership from a trait perspective?
- Your team specializes in leadership from a behavioral perspective?
- Your team specializes in leadership from a contingency perspective?

- Think about the concepts of transformational leadership and servant leadership. How are they similar and how are they different? Could a leader be considered transformational and servant at the same time?
- Can you think of a case when a leader might choose not to be authentic in a leadership situation for the sake of their followers? How could they reconcile their lack of authenticity with their leadership values?

Notes

1 Reagan, R. (1975, December 14). Interview with Mike Wallace. *60 Minutes*. CBS.
2 Tsu, S. (1910). *The Art of War* (L. Giles, Trans.). London: The Puppet Press.
3 Stogdill, R. M. (1948). Personal factors associated with leadership: A survey of the literature. *Journal of Psychology*, 25(1), 35–71.
4 Vroom, V. H., & Yetton, P. W. (1973). *Leadership and Decision Making*. University of Pittsburgh Press.
5 Selznick, P. (1957). *Leadership in Administration: A Sociological Interpretation*. Harper & Row.
6 Herzberg, F., Mausner, B., & Snyderman, B. B. (1959). *The Motivation to Work*. John Wiley & Sons.
7 Fiedler, F. E. (1964). A contingency model of leadership effectiveness. In L. Berkowitz (Ed.), *Advances in Experimental Social Psychology* (Vol. 1, pp. 149–190). Academic Press.
8 House, R. J. (1971). A path-goal theory of leader effectiveness. *Administrative Science Quarterly*, 16(3), 321–339.
9 Greenleaf, R. K. (1970). The servant as leader. Retrieved from https://www.greenleaf.org/what-is-servant-leadership/
10 Sendjaya, S., & Sarros, J. C. (2002). Servant leadership: Its origin, development, and application in organizations. *Journal of Leadership & Organizational Studies*, 9(2), 57–64.
11 Greenleaf, R. K. (1977). *Servant Leadership: A Journey into the Nature of Legitimate Power and Greatness*. Paulist Press.

12 Sendjaya, S., & Sarros, J. C. (2002). Servant leadership: Its origin, development, and application in organizations. *Journal of Leadership & Organizational Studies*, 9(2), 57–64.
13 Burns, J. M. (1978). *Leadership*. Harper & Row.
14 Bass, B. M. (1985). *Leadership and Performance beyond Expectations*. Free Press.
15 Bass, B. M. (1985). *Leadership and Performance beyond Expectations*. Free Press.
16 Avolio, B. J., Zhu, W., Koh, W., & Bhatia, P. (2004). Transformational leadership and organizational commitment: Mediating role of psychological empowerment and moderating role of structural distance. *Journal of Organizational Behavior*, 25(8), 951–968.
17 Judge, T. A., & Piccolo, R. F. (2004). Transformational and transactional leadership: A meta-analytic test of their relative validity. *Journal of Applied Psychology*, 89(5), 755–768.
18 Kelley, R. E. (1992). *The Power of Followership*. New York: Doubleday.
19 Uhl-Bien, M., Riggio, R. E., Lowe, K. B., & Carsten, M. K. (2014). Followership theory: A review and research agenda. *The Leadership Quarterly*, 25(1), 83–104.
20 Bass, B. M. (2008). *The Bass Handbook of Leadership: Theory, Research, and Managerial Applications* (4th ed.). Free Press.
21 Kelley, R. E. (1992). *The Power of Followership*. New York: Doubleday.
22 Uhl-Bien, M., Riggio, R. E., Lowe, K. B., & Carsten, M. K. (2014). Followership theory: A review and research agenda. *The Leadership Quarterly*, 25(1), 83–104.
23 Avolio, B. J., & Gardner, W. L. (2005). Authentic leadership development: Getting to the root of positive forms of leadership. *The Leadership Quarterly*, 16(3), 315–338.
24 Walumbwa, F. O., Avolio, B. J., Gardner, W. L., Wernsing, T. S., & Peterson, S. J. (2008). Authentic leadership: Development and validation of a theory-based measure. *Journal of Management*, 34(1), 89–126.

Part II

Building the leadership role

The SPACE model

Peter Brook, the legendary British theater director, was known for his unconventional and thought-provoking productions of Shakespeare's plays. In his book *The Empty Space*,[1] he suggests that any space can become a stage for theater, emphasizing that the essence of theater is not in its physical setting but in the act of performance itself. When an actor performs and someone watches, that interaction transforms any space into a stage. This metaphor of *The Empty Space* is about the potential of simple elements coming together to create something profound and impactful.

In the context of leadership, the potential and opportunity within every leadership scenario can be compared to Brook's "empty space." The leader, just like the performer, steps into this space armed with key skills to inspire followers to achieve a shared goal. Leadership qualities such as self-awareness, presence, authenticity, communication, and emotional intelligence transform the "empty space" of daily leadership challenges into opportunities for meaningful interaction, growth, and impact. This metaphor highlights the transformative power of leadership, just as Brook emphasizes the transformative power of theater.

In this book, we assume that effective leadership is based on five key qualities: self-awareness, presence, authenticity, communication, and emotional intelligence. The acronym SPACE summarizes these essential qualities and serves as a way to structure the rest of the book. The relevance of self-awareness in leadership is fundamental for leaders to recognize their own strengths and

DOI: 10.4324/9781003349815-5

weaknesses, a critical component for personal growth and effective leadership. Similarly, presence is a key element for leaders to command respect and attention effectively. Authenticity—being true to one's values and beliefs, is indispensable for earning trust and inspiring follower loyalty. Effective communication is essential for driving team alignment and decision-making. Lastly, emotional intelligence allows leaders to manage their emotions well, which makes them more successful at navigating the complexities of their leadership roles and environments.

In the upcoming chapters, we will explore the key leadership skills contained in the SPACE model. Each chapter will delve into one of these skills, offering theoretical foundations, practical insights, examples, and exercises on the integration of acting techniques and leadership development.

Note

1 Brook, P. (1968). *The Empty Space.* Touchstone.

4 Self-awareness

In Shakespeare's *Julius Caesar*, Cassius, who is trying to persuade Brutus to join a conspiracy against Caesar, says "The fault, dear Brutus, is not in our stars, but in ourselves, that we are underlings."[1] With this line, Cassius challenges the notion of fate controlling their lives. He argues that it is their own actions and decisions that have led them to be subordinate to Caesar. This moment underscores a central theme of the play: the tension between destiny and free will. Cassius' argument is that their status and future are not predetermined by some cosmic force (represented metaphorically by the "stars"), but are the results of their own choices and actions.

Cassius' line resonates well with the concept of self-awareness in the context of leadership development. Self-awareness involves understanding one's own character, feelings, motives, and desires. The quote suggests that our circumstances, successes, and failures are often the result of our own actions and choices, rather than fate or destiny. Just as Cassius suggests that they are not meant to be underlings, but are so due to their own choices, self-awareness in leadership means knowing oneself, so that we can take responsibility for our own actions and decisions.

The SPACE model underscores self-awareness as the first step in leadership development. Acknowledging and understanding one's own strengths and weaknesses marks the beginning of a journey of introspection and personal accountability. These are both essential elements for personal growth and effective leadership.

Who am I?

The famous American acting teacher and actress, Uta Hagen, articulates the significance of the question "Who Am I?" as the

DOI: 10.4324/9781003349815-6

first step in creating a character. This question, which resonates deeply in both the worlds of acting and leadership, serves as a guiding light for understanding and embracing one's true self.

Hagen teaches actors to explore their character's history, looking at their life stories and at how their beliefs have changed. Leaders do something similar by looking back at their own lives, including the good and bad experiences that have made them who they are today. This helps them see what drives them as people and as leaders.

Actors who understand themselves can give more realistic and convincing performances given that they are able to draw real traits, behaviors, and emotions from their own lives. They can also easily understand the ways in which their characters are like them, and different from them. Leaders who do the same can connect more honestly with others. By being true to themselves, they are able to foster open communication, empathy, and trust among their followers.

In addition to better understanding their roles by asking themselves who they are as characters, self-aware actors are also better equipped to deliver convincing and authentic performances by leveraging their range, voice, and physical abilities to portray a character effectively. By recognizing their limitations and working on improving them, actors can improve their craft and deliver exceptional performances. Similarly, leaders who have undergone the process of self-awareness become better at connecting genuinely.

Purpose

Purpose is about the "why" behind your actions or the reason for your existence. It is your core identity and what drives you as an individual or an organization. In Uta Hagen's acting technique, purpose is included in the question: "Who am I?" It is deeply personal and often enduring, serving as a guiding principle for decision-making and goal-setting. It answers questions like "What is my reason for being?" or "What is my true calling?"

In a *Harvard Business Review* article, Nick Craig and Scott Snook[2] argue that purpose-driven leadership has gained significant traction, recognized as a key element in exceptional leadership, superior performance, and greater well-being. The idea that a leader's most crucial role is to be a steward of their organization's purpose has been promoted by academics, while business experts argue that purpose is the linchpin of exceptional performance. Psychologists also highlight how purpose can lead to greater personal well-being. Even doctors have found that individuals with a sense of purpose tend to be less prone to disease.

However, despite the growing recognition of the importance of purpose in leadership, a significant challenge persists. Studies conducted among leaders reveal that fewer than 20% possess a strong sense of their own individual purpose. Even fewer can articulate this purpose in a clear and concrete statement. While many leaders can readily articulate their organization's mission, their own purpose often remains vague and generic, encompassing broad ideals like "helping others excel" or "ensuring success." Moreover, many leaders lack a coherent plan for translating their purpose into meaningful action. This deficiency often limits their ambitions and results in the failure to achieve their most ambitious professional and personal goals.

Discovering one's leadership purpose is not as easy as it may sound. In a world that bombards us with messages about who we should be and how we should lead, understanding who you truly are can be a daunting task. It requires introspection and reflection, which can be uncomfortable and challenging for some. However, the process of finding your purpose is a critical step towards personal and professional growth.

To craft a purpose statement that resonates deeply, leaders must draw from their life experiences, identifying common threads and major themes that represent their core strengths, values, and passions. It is through this introspective exploration that a unique purpose statement begins to take shape. This statement is personal, specific, and deeply reflective of who you are. It is a call to action, encapsulating your essence and motivating you to live it out.

Self-aware leaders

The case of Satya Nadella, the CEO of Microsoft, is a good example of a self-aware leader. When Nadella took over as CEO in

2014, Microsoft was struggling to keep up with the rapid changes in the technology industry, and the company's market share and revenue had been declining. Nadella recognized that Microsoft needed a significant shift in its culture and strategy to stay relevant, and he understood that this change had to start with him. He began by taking a deep dive into his own leadership style and identifying his strengths and weaknesses. He also sought feedback from his colleagues and employees to gain a better understanding of how his leadership was perceived.

Through this process of self-reflection and self-awareness, Nadella was able to identify areas where he needed to improve and develop his leadership skills. For example, he recognized that he needed to be more empathetic and to listen more to his employees' ideas and concerns. He also realized that he needed to be more comfortable with taking risks and experimenting with new ideas, rather than relying solely on traditional approaches.[3]

Consider also the remarkable example of the late Anita Roddick, the visionary founder of The Body Shop. In the early 1970s, at a time when ethical and socially responsible business practices were far from mainstream, Roddick embarked on a journey of self-awareness that led her to embrace these principles with unwavering conviction.[4]

Her story begins in the mid-1960s, when Roddick herself was embracing the hippie lifestyle, a period that laid the groundwork for her later business philosophy. In 1976, she opened the first Body Shop in Brighton, not just as a means of income but as a platform for her evolving ideas about ethical consumerism. She knew who she was and wanted to make sure that her business reflected her values and beliefs. Her products, notably different from the traditional offerings of the cosmetic industry, were not tested on animals, a practice that was then standard worldwide.

Roddick's role in getting cosmetic testing on animals banned in Britain, and later in Europe, exemplifies the potential of business to provoke social change, especially when it is grounded in real values and beliefs. It highlighted her understanding that a business could be a powerful tool for societal transformation. This insight was revolutionary, especially in a time when the idea of businesses being a force for social good was largely unimagined.

Additionally, Roddick was a pioneer in the fair trade movement. She not only sourced products ethically but also ensured that producers in developing countries received fair compensation. This practice ran counter to the exploitative tendencies of Western capitalism and helped shift consumer consciousness towards more ethically produced goods. Roddick's approach to fair trade was not just about doing business differently; it was about fairness and supporting human rights globally.

Roddick's self-awareness allowed her to challenge the norms of the business world and demonstrated that capitalism, in the right hands, could be a force for good, repairing damages it had previously caused. Roddick's approach encouraged other social entrepreneurs to rethink the role of business in society, showing that companies could be successful while also being socially and environmentally responsible.

Leadership crucibles

In our efforts to truly know ourselves and our leadership styles, we have to be aware of the events in our lives that shaped who we are today. These events are often referred to as leadership crucibles. According to Warren Bennis and Robert J. Thomas,[5] who coined the term, leadership crucibles are transformative life events that profoundly influence a leader's development. These are not just challenging experiences but defining moments that forge a leader's identity and perspective. They are events that leaders cite in their leadership narratives as pivotal moments in their leadership journeys.

The essence of these crucibles lies in their ability to drive leaders toward deep self-reflection. They present circumstances that challenge leaders' deepest values and beliefs, fostering a heightened sense of identity and self-awareness. This introspection is crucial, as understanding one's motivations, strengths, and weaknesses is essential for effective leadership.

One of the key aspects of leadership crucibles is learning from adversity. Leaders often emerge from these challenging situations with resilience, adaptability, and an ability to maintain composure under pressure. These experiences teach invaluable lessons about perseverance and the importance of staying true to one's values in the face of obstacles. Furthermore, these crucibles often instill a deeper sense of empathy and understanding in leaders. Those who have overcome significant challenges tend to develop an enhanced ability to connect with and inspire their teams. This empathetic approach is a critical component of self-aware leadership.

As leaders, it is important that we think of leadership crucibles not only as merely challenges to be endured, but rather as opportunities for growth and self-discovery. As leaders, we should embrace these experiences, reflect on them, and integrate the lessons learned into our leadership style and narrative. Developing resilience to bounce back from adversity and cultivating empathy and understanding are critical for long-term leadership effectiveness. Leadership crucibles, therefore, play a pivotal role in shaping who we are as leaders.

Embracing our leadership crucibles

Delving into one's life and looking for crucibles can be a vulnerable experience. It's a process that may unearth moments of cognitive dissonance, where our professed values seem at odds with our actions. However, this exploration is an essential step in the journey of self-awareness. It is through embracing our leadership crucibles that we can shed the masks we may have worn to conform to societal or organizational expectations.

Let's take a look at the example of Oprah Winfrey, the iconic American media mogul, television host, and philanthropist. From her modest beginnings in rural Mississippi to her global recognition, Oprah's narrative illustrates the strength that emerges from recognizing and embracing crucibles, laying the foundation for genuine and influential leadership.

Oprah's journey began with the profound acknowledgment of vulnerability in her own life. Born into poverty in rural Mississippi, she faced significant adversity from a young age. Raised by her grandmother, she experienced not only financial hardship but also emotional and physical abuse. Oprah openly shares these deeply personal experiences, including the trauma of sexual abuse, with her audience.

Her vulnerability in discussing these painful aspects of her past allowed her to create a powerful narrative to connect with her viewers. By openly sharing her struggles, Oprah demonstrated that vulnerability could be a source of strength and connection rather than weakness. She transformed her life challenges into crucibles that shaped her leadership.

Her journey also involved deep reflection on her core values and beliefs. She recognized that her mission was to use her platform for positive change, to empower individuals, and to promote empathy and understanding. These values became the guiding principles of her leadership. Her reflection also extended to understanding the value of storytelling and authentic communication. Oprah believed that the stories behind her leadership crucibles had the power to change lives.

In her efforts to align her actions with her values, Oprah launched numerous initiatives and campaigns focused on education, literacy, and empowerment. Her commitment to these causes went beyond public appearances; she used her influence and resources to make a tangible difference in the lives of others. Her willingness to embrace vulnerability and share her journey has inspired millions of individuals around the world.

Oprah Winfrey's personal journey exemplifies the transformative power of embracing crucibles in leadership. By acknowledging vulnerability, reflecting on values, and aligning actions with principles of empathy and positive change, she has not only led authentically but also inspired a generation of leaders to do the same.

Writing our own autobiography

Hagen's profound insight into character development in acting resonates deeply in the context of leadership and self-awareness. Hagen emphasizes the need for an actor to create a new autobiography for their character, one that breathes life into their role, infusing it with authenticity and depth. In much the same way, crafting our own life autobiography is a transformative exercise that can help us as leaders to uncover our core values and beliefs, laying the foundation for authentic leadership.

This exercise is not merely about recounting life events, but a profound introspection into the essence of our being. Here, we will explore a structured approach to writing our own autobiographies, a journey that promises self-discovery and a deeper understanding of our values and beliefs. These five steps will provide you with a solid foundation for writing your own autobiography.

1. **Begin with reflection:** dedicate time to introspection. Consider your life journey, from early childhood to the present. Reflect on pivotal moments, experiences, and relationships that have shaped you. Take note of significant milestones, challenges, and achievements. This initial step sets the stage for a comprehensive self-exploration.

2. **Identify influential figures:** recall the individuals who have had a significant impact on your life. These could be family members, mentors, friends, or even public figures. Explore how their values, beliefs, and actions may have influenced your own perspective and principles.

3. **Values and beliefs inventory:** create a list of values and beliefs that you hold dear. These may encompass principles such as integrity, empathy, social responsibility, innovation, or any other guiding philosophy that resonates with you. Reflect on the origins of these values—whether they were instilled by upbringing, shaped by experiences, or developed through personal reflection.

4. **Signature stories:** identify the stories or experiences from your life that have left a lasting imprint on your values and beliefs. These are your "signature stories"—narratives that define who you are and what you stand for. Share these stories with others to provide context for your leadership style and decisions.

5. **Alignment assessment:** evaluate the alignment between your values and beliefs and your actions as a leader. Are your decisions and behaviors congruent with your core principles? Identify areas where alignment is strong and areas where adjustments may be needed to lead authentically.

By engaging in this process of writing our own autobiography, we can embark on a transformative journey of self-awareness. Writing a clear autobiography allows us to uncover the foundations of our leadership—our values and beliefs—and gain a deeper understanding of the essence of our being. This newfound clarity empowers us, as leaders, to make decisions with integrity, inspire our teams, and create environments where individuals thrive, teams excel, and organizations make a meaningful impact on the world.

Exploring our inner-monologues

One of the best ways to get to know who we really are and how we really feel about something or someone is by exploring our inner thoughts and emotions in a monologue. This exploration allows us to gain greater self-awareness and a deeper understanding of our emotional responses to different situations or people.

Like with the autobiography, we will introduce here a structured approach to create our inner-monologues. Whether you are driving your car or taking a shower, inner-monologues are a wonderful way to explore who you really are and your leadership style.

1. **Setting the stage:** create a scenario where you play a role you're familiar with, like one from your job. Imagine real situations and people, like discussing a team member's performance if you're a department head.
2. **Performing the monologue:** find a quiet spot, like your car or shower, to carry out this monologue. Talk to yourself about this person, sharing your thoughts and feelings about them. Be detailed in explaining why you feel this way. You can record yourself.
3. **Reflecting:** after the monologue, think about the emotions you felt. What were your first thoughts and reactions? If you recorded yourself, listen to the monologue and pay attention to how you feel when you listen to it.
4. **Analyzing:** consider how this inner talk could affect how you act and decide things about this co-worker. Reflect honestly on this.
5. **Take-aways:** ponder how this exercise can boost your self-awareness as a leader. How can understanding your emotions and thoughts better help you be more effective at work?

The exercise can be modified to focus on specific scenarios or leadership challenges that are relevant to you. It can be repeated multiple times to help you gain greater insight into your own emotional responses and thought patterns, and to help you develop a deeper understanding of your own leadership style.

A unique and dynamic journey

Expanding on the journey to self-awareness, it's important to recognize that this path is unique for every individual. It requires us to be introspective, to regularly pause and reflect on our actions, decisions, and their impacts. This self-reflection isn't always easy. It often involves facing uncomfortable truths about ourselves, acknowledging our flaws, and working toward change. But it's in this process of honest self-evaluation that we grow as leaders.

This journey also involves understanding how others perceive us. Feedback from colleagues and team members can provide valuable insights. It's about listening, not just to respond, but to understand and evolve. As leaders, our actions and words have a significant impact on those around us. By becoming more self-aware, we can ensure this impact is positive and inspiring.

Moreover, self-awareness leads to better decision-making. When we understand our biases and triggers, we can make choices that are more thoughtful and considerate. This not only benefits us personally but also enhances the effectiveness and harmony of our teams.

Finally, remember that self-awareness is a continuous process. There is no final destination. As we evolve, so do our insights about ourselves. Each day offers a new opportunity to learn, grow, and lead more effectively. Embracing this journey with an open heart and mind will not only enrich our leadership but also our lives.

Conclusion

Self-awareness isn't just about knowing what we like or dislike; it's a deeper understanding of the values and beliefs that define who we are. This chapter highlighted how important this understanding is for leaders. We looked at how leaders like Satya Nadella and Anita Roddick used self-awareness to make big changes in their leadership styles and the cultures of their organizations. These stories show us that knowing ourselves can really transform the way we lead.

The chapter also introduced the idea of "leadership crucibles." These are major events or experiences that have a big impact on how we lead. We discussed that being self-aware is an ongoing journey, not a single event. It's about continuously reflecting on ourselves, listening to feedback from others, and making sure our actions line up with our deepest values. This constant process of reflection and learning is key to growing and becoming more effective leaders.

Reflective questions

1. Think about a defining moment in your leadership journey. How did this experience change your perspective on leadership and your understanding of yourself?
2. What aspects of your life or work give you the most fulfillment and a sense of purpose? How can you incorporate more of those elements into your leadership?
3. Identify a leadership crucible in your life. What were the key lessons, and how have they influenced your approach to leading others?
4. Analyze how well your actions as a leader align with your core values. Identify areas of congruence and divergence, and consider strategies for better alignment.
5. Examine your decision-making process in a recent critical situation. How did your self-awareness influence the outcome, and what insights did you gain about your leadership strengths and areas for improvement?

Notes

1 Shakespeare, W. (1599). *Julius Caesar*.
2 Craig N. & Snook S. (2014, May). From purpose to impact. *Harvard Business Review*.
3 Nadella, S. (2017). *Hit Refresh: The Quest to Rediscover Microsoft's Soul and Imagine a Better Future for Everyone*. HarperBusiness.
4 *The Independent*. (2007, September 12). How Anita changed the world. Retrieved from https://www.independent.co.uk/.
5 Bennis, W. G., & Thomas, R. J. (2002). Crucibles of leadership. *Harvard Business Review*, 80(9), 39–45.

5   Presence

Stella Adler, one of the most important figures in the American theater and mentor to some of the most iconic actors, including Marlon Brando, Robert De Niro, and Warren Beatty, believed that an actor's presence on stage should be so profound and commanding that it should feel as if they were addressing the entire world. This concept of presence goes beyond mere physicality; it's about conveying significance, strength, and conviction. One of her most famous quotes reflects this idea perfectly: "When you stand on the stage, you must have a sense that you are addressing the whole world, and that what you say is so important the whole world must listen."[1]

When we see a leader addressing their followers, in an office, a conference room, or an auditorium, we can tell right away if the person has presence. Take the example of Barack Obama, president of the United States between 2008 and 2016. In 2004, when he was just a junior senator for the state of Illinois and practically unknown to the general public, he delivered an electrifying speech at the Democratic National Convention in support of John Kerry's nomination for the presidential election. In this historic speech, Obama captured the audience thanks to a combination of rhetorical tools, performance elements, and especially his stage presence. The speech gained the young senator national recognition and pave the way for his nomination as the Democratic presidential candidate in 2008.[2] Many other speeches and public appearances followed. In all we see Obama's capacity to communicate effectively, with an extraordinary leadership presence.

In the theater, stage presence refers to an actor's ability to command the attention of an audience. We can tell an actor has presence the moment they walk on stage. They don't really have to say a word for us to feel their stage presence. They could just be standing there, looking away, or even sitting without talking.

DOI: 10.4324/9781003349815-7

They could be dressed in very simple clothes or even naked. Presence goes beyond what the actor says or wears. But is presence something that we are born with, or can it be acquired? Is presence the same thing as charisma, or is it something else? Can anyone, including leaders, develop presence?

In its simplest definition, presence refers to being present in a place. Thus, someone who attends a meeting is said to be present. However, in the sense of stage presence, being present is not enough. The actor also has to be connected with what is happening in the external environment as well as with their inner thoughts. It involves a state of complete alertness. The actor has to be there, at that specific time, living moment to moment, connecting with the circumstances of the play, and feeling the audience.

Although presence is mainly perceived through external elements such as posture, body movements, or facial expression, its essence lies in the actor's capacity to express their inner selves through those external elements. When the actor's inner life is in synch with their expressiveness and the circumstances of the play, and the actor is living in the moment, we say that they have stage presence.

Audiences often feel that actors possess a certain innate charisma, which allows them to have stage presence. However, in most cases, this quality is not innate but rather something actors develop over time. In this sense, charisma and presence are different. The former is often thought of as an innate quality, while the latter is considered a learned skill. In this book, we assume that leaders can develop presence the same way actors develop stage presence. We are not going to cover charisma, as this is a quality that is often perceived as innate and, in principle could not be developed. Our focus will be on presence.

Leadership presence

We can define leadership presence as the capacity that a leader has to be present, in the moment, completely connected to their own thoughts, able to express their feelings, and very aware of their surroundings. This means that to develop presence, leaders have to learn how to connect with their thoughts while being completely open to the outside world. This, of course, is easier said than done. We tend to think of presence as being able to command the attention of others. But that's only the outcome.

Belle Linda Halpern and Kathy Lubar,[3] both actors and leadership coaches, have created a model of leadership presence based on their many years of experience in both leadership coaching and theater performance. Their model, which provides a useful and systematic way to teach and learn leadership presence, distinguishes four essential elements that leaders need to develop in order to have leadership presence. They use the acronym PRES to name their model. Thus, P stands for being present (completely in the moment and ready to react to the unexpected), R stands for reaching out (capacity to build relations, to be empathetic and make connections with others), E stands for expressiveness (ability to express one's feelings and emotions), and S stands for self-knowledge (knowledge and acceptance of the self, with honesty and authenticity).

Being present does not come easy to everyone. Although we are born with this capacity, we tend to lose it as we grow up. We become more concerned with the future or the past rather than with the present. We have difficulties focusing and connecting with our inner thoughts. Our imagination diminishes as well as our ability to freely connect with our emotions and express our feelings.

Babies and small children can do it with no effort. They are able to be here, in this moment, totally alert. They are neither in the past nor in the future; they are always in the present. They easily connect with their inner thoughts and imagination. And when something upsets them or makes them happy, they react right away accordingly and express their emotions freely.

In a world in which we are constantly distracted by our electronic devices, being present has become more challenging than ever. We check messages and read emails in meetings, classrooms, and conferences, we often look at social media postings and update our profiles in the middle of our workday, we spend too much time taking pictures and posting them on our accounts rather than fully enjoying a holiday or a vacation with friends and family. Our thoughts are often in the future or in the past instead of the present. Our attention span and levels of concentration seem to become shorter and shorter every day.

How can we improve our capacity to be present? The obvious answer would be to pay more attention to others, to focus more on what's happening in front of us, and to always listen carefully and make eye contact when having conversations. But there are some techniques that we can borrow from the theater to help us be more present. Below we will describe four of them: belly breathing, neutral position, mirror exercise, and improvisations.

Belly breathing

The purpose of this technique is to learn how to breathe with your belly, so that you can relax, be completely present, and live in the moment. Being relaxed is likely to make you more alert to anything around you, more creative, and a better decision maker. Also, after learning how to breathe with your belly, you should be able to use this technique every time you need to be completely focused and in control. This includes stressful situations in which you need to overcome fear and anxiety such as speaking in public, giving presentations, or attending important interviews and meetings.

Although as babies we breathe with our bellies, many of us develop a bad habit of breathing with our chests as we grow older. This often prevents us from relaxing and projecting our voices properly. It puts unnecessary tension on our hearts and causes stress. In fact, several studies suggest that anxiety, depression, and even heart disease could be linked to chest breathing behaviors.[4] When you look at a baby sleeping, you will notice the belly rising and falling as they breathe. This is precisely the way we should breathe.

It can be difficult to find your belly breathing, especially after years and years of chest breathing. A good way to start is by sitting in a chair, with the back straight against the chair, both feet grounded on the floor, one hand on your chest and the other one on your belly. Before paying attention to your breathing, you should make sure that your whole body is completely relaxed.

There are several ways to do this. You might already have a technique that works well for you. One possible way is as follows: after closing your eyes, start contracting each part of your body for a couple of seconds and then releasing it. You should only do one part at a time. You can start with your toes and move gradually upwards until you reach your head. Make sure you cover only one part at a time, including each toe, your ankles, knees, lower and upper legs, your pelvis, torso, each finger, hands, lower and upper arms, back, shoulders, neck, mouth, ears, nose, eyes, and scalp. After having done each and every part of your body, you should feel completely relaxed.

Once you are relaxed, you should start focusing your attention on your breathing. If your breathing is in the chest, try to move it down to the belly. The hand that sits on the belly should be the one rising every time you inhale, and falling every time you exhale. Try to inhale through your nose and exhale through your mouth. Make sure you breathe deeply, trying to fill up your lungs completely. You might not be able to achieve belly breathing the first few times you try this exercise. However, you should practice every day until belly breathing becomes second nature.

It is important to note that belly breathing can be checked anytime during the day when you need to feel relaxed. It is always a good idea to take a short break once a day to practice it. Also, when you are working, you can test your belly breathing skills. This will relax you and will allow you to focus your attention on the present moment and make you more efficient.

Belly breathing is a technique used by actors, singers, and dancers alike. It allows them to relax and have complete control of their bodies while performing. Once you master this technique, you will certainly improve your leadership presence and communication skills.

Neutral position

The neutral position refers to an aligned posture in which the body is completely balanced and relaxed. This position is important in the performing arts as it allows artists to use it as a starting point when expressing themselves with their bodies. The key to the neutral position is to find a relaxed posture following the body's line of gravity. That is to say, the position of the body should follow an imaginary vertical line running from the ground all the way to the top of the head. Like performers, leaders need to master this position so that they can be relaxed enough in order to use their bodies to express themselves.

The neutral position can be described as follows: while standing straight, and with both feet firmly planted on the floor and slightly separated on a horizontal line, legs, arms, and hands are relaxed, neck is straight, shoulders are aligned horizontally, and the spine is aligned vertically, as if being pulled by a string from the ceiling. Eyes are looking directly ahead. There are no tensions in joints, neck, shoulders, or spine. There is a feeling of relaxation, as if any part of the body could be moved by the wind. The breathing happens through the belly, as described in the previous section.

Leaders need to master the neutral position so that they can move smoothly and convey assurance. In a way, the neutral position is a position of power as it shows that the person is in total control of the body and ready to move when necessary. It also allows the person to take control of the space in a smooth manner, the same way an actor, singer, or dancer moves swiftly and with assurance on stage.

President Obama's posture while standing is generally a good example of an optimal neutral position. This is more evident in the final years of his presidency. Standing straight and relaxed allows him to rotate smoothly when addressing crowds or in press conferences. This position also allows him to move with assurance and grace, conveying total control of his own body and the space in which he moves.

Mirror exercise

The mirror exercise is widely used in acting training. One of its main purposes is to allow actors to be completely present, in the moment, totally responsive to their partners. Viola Spolin, the legendary American acting teacher, popularized this exercise in her seminal book Improvisation for the theater in 1963.[5]

The exercise has three phases. In the first phase, actors pair off and decide who is going to lead and who is going to follow. They face each other, and those who lead start moving their bodies while those who follow try to be their exact mirror. If the leader moves the left leg, then the follower moves the right leg, if the leader moves the right arm, then the follower moves the left arm. This goes on for a few minutes until the actors are totally in synch. The exercise becomes a synchronized dance.

In phase two, actors reverse roles. The leader becomes the follower and the follower the leader. They repeat the mirroring for a few minutes until they are completely in synch again. In the final phase, the actors switch roles while they are mirroring each other. There is no pre-determined leader or follower. This is the most challenging and interesting phase as partners really have to focus on each other, making sure that they mirror each other perfectly and that they know when to follow and when to lead.

Sometimes, when the two partners are completely connected, it is almost impossible to tell who is leading and who is following. They move in total harmony as if they were partners in a smooth and synchronized dance. When this happens, it is truly magical. It shows that both partners are completely present, living moment to moment, without anticipating anything.

The mirror exercise is often followed by a group discussion. There are several relevant questions to leadership which can emerge from the exercise: was there cooperation between the two partners, or was there competition? Did one partner act as leader more often than the other? How comfortable did each partner feel when following the other? How did each one feel when leading the other? How alert did they seem? Were they able to be in the moment, or were they trying to anticipate each other's moves?

Besides these leadership-related questions, it is also interesting to discuss other aspects which can emerge from this exercise. For example, did the execution of the exercise convey a story? Was there a conflict? Was there a resolution? The mirror exercise offers endless possibilities for both artists and leaders. Practicing the exercise will help you to be more present, more responsive to others, and more aware of what's happening around you. These are all essential qualities in the leadership process.

Improvisations

In the theater, improvisations refer to role-playing exercises in which participants neither prepare the scene beforehand nor follow a script. This requires the actors to be totally present, living moment to moment, listening to each other. They cannot anticipate what they are going to say or do, as they don't know in advance what the other actor is going to say or do. The required level of alertness on the actors' part is very high. Chapter 9 covers improvisation and its connection to leadership in detail.

How does an improvisation work? After establishing a dramatic situation (a situation where there is a conflict) and defining the actors' roles, the time of the scene, and the place, each participant (usually two at the beginning of the improvisation) chooses an objective (what they want from the other character). These objectives are often conflicting objectives so that there is a real dramatic situation. For example, if the given situation takes place in an office, one actor, playing the boss, might want to fire the other actor, playing the employee. The employee's objective might be to keep his job. Similarly, if the situation takes place in a home between a wife and a husband, the wife might want a divorce while the husband might want to save the marriage.

The main rule that any actor has to keep in mind when improvising is that whatever the other actor says becomes a reality. The actor is expected to build on it. They can't deny or contradict what the other actor establishes. In addition, like in any other acting exercise, it is important that actors really believe in who they are as characters, what they want from each other, and the established circumstances of the situation.

Due to the lack of preparation in improvisations and the impossibility of contradicting what the other actor establishes, the exercise requires participants to be completely present, in the moment, really listening to each other. This is precisely what makes improvisations such a useful exercise when leaders work on listening and being present.

Improvisations are often used in acting as warm-up exercises, or to allow actors to become familiar with the circumstances of the play. In this respect, directors often ask actors to improvise the previous circumstances of the play (what happened before the beginning of the scene). This allows them to explore scenes that are not written in the script. Also, when actors can't grasp the essence of a scene, directors often ask them to improvise it. This tends to bring up many different aspects of the scene that actors were not able to see when reading, analyzing, and rehearsing the script. Also, improvisations give actors the freedom to experience real emotions without having to worry about knowing the lines.

From a leadership development perspective, improvisations can also be used to allow leaders to explore various leadership styles. The dramatic situation can be set up in a way that gives them the opportunity to try different leadership approaches, which they wouldn't normally apply. Also, the exercise allows leaders to experience being followers. You will find these improvisation exercises very useful not only to be more present and learn how to listen to each other, but also to know yourself and the kind of leader you are or aspire to be.

Practicing presence

1. **Belly breathing:** read the section above on the breathing exercise and practice it at home. Make sure to eliminate all possible distractions while working on the exercise. If you find yourself very distracted, focus your attention on your breathing, its movement, and its sound. After completing the exercise, take notes on your level of concentration and presence during the exercise. Repeat it every day and take notes until you feel that your level of concentration and presence has improved. If you are using this book for a course, be ready to share your experience in class.

2. **Neutral position**: observe one leader or public speaker, either in person or on the Internet, when addressing an audience. Pay close attention to the body's position. Is this person adopting the neutral position? If so, how can you tell? If not, what could this person do to improve the body's position?
3. **Moving from the neutral position**: stand in front of a full-length mirror until you feel you have achieved the neutral position. Rotate your body from that position as if addressing an audience in an amphitheater. Use your right arm to indicate something on an imaginary board and bring it back to the neutral position. Then repeat the same movement with your left arm. Movements should be smooth and should require minimum effort.

Voice and diction

Now that we have discussed key elements related to presence such as breathing and posture, we turn our focus to the importance of voice and diction in leadership. This section highlights how a clear and confident voice is crucial for effective leadership communication. We first look at the importance of mastering the voice and projecting it. Then we discuss good diction and its significance for leaders to convey their messages clearly and to support a strong and commanding presence.

Mastering the voice

Together with body and language, voice allows leaders to express themselves. The voice refers to the sound produced in the larynx of a person and uttered through the mouth. Like singers and actors, leaders need to take care of their voices, as they are key to the process of inspiring followers to pursue and achieve common goals.

Mastering the voice implies being able to control its tones in order to produce variety. It also involves learning how to project it so that it can be heard. Although nowadays conference rooms and amphitheaters are often equipped with microphones, learning how to project the voice also contributes to making it fuller. A good projected voice conveys assurance, control, and respect. Also, mastering the voice involves having good diction. That is to say, having the capacity to pronounce words clearly.

The first step when trying to master the voice is relaxation. Breathing through the belly and keeping a neutral position are fundamental elements when trying to produce a full and rich voice. We have all experienced our voices breaking in moments of excessive tension or nervousness. It is through relaxation, which starts from breathing properly, that we can master our voices. In fact, the best way to overcome nerves during an interview or a presentation is by taking deep breaths through the belly.

A monotone speech is one of the biggest obstacles in oral communication. After listening to someone with little or no variety in the voice, we tend to stop paying attention to what is being said. The voice is probably one of the richest instruments when it comes to producing different tones and sounds. Not taking advantage of this amazing feature is simply a waste of resources.

Although it takes singers and actors years to master their voices, there are a few techniques that we can apply to add some variety to our voices. First of all, we can vary the pitch and volume of our voices, or the speed of what we say, according to the meaning of what we are trying to communicate. We can stress points by increasing the tone of the voice or reducing the speed of the speech, making sure we clearly pronounce all words. This is likely to put emphasis on what we say. We can also use pauses to give variety to the voice and stress meaning.

For example, a priest or a minister who, after introducing a thought, calls for his congregation's reflection, and pauses to give them time to reflect, is also using this pause as a way to stress its importance. Similarly, a coach who accelerates the speed of her speech and raises the volume of her voice when trying to energize the team, is also using these tools to stress the urgency of the situation.

As mentioned before, the meaning of what we say is rarely based on what has been said, but rather about how it was said. The same sentence can be said in various different ways, expressing different meanings every time. For instance, telling someone "I love you" can mean "I can't live without you" if said with passion or can mean "I like you" if said casually but with warmth or can mean "I hate you" if said with enough irony and disdain.

Projecting the voice requires a relaxed body and good breathing habits. The energy to project the voice far and wide comes from the bottom of the belly. Although the sound is always produced in the larynx, the force to produce this sound should come from the belly to maximize the projection of the voice. This also prevents yelling, which can damage the vocal cords.

Being able to control their breath and project their voices are essential skills for singers and actors. When they breathe with their bellies, the air is used to control the desired volume. The sound produced has a certain texture of a rich, full, and deep quality. It is very different from the sound that comes from someone who is yelling, which is rather flat and has an acute pitch.

The "ha" exercise is a useful voice technique which actors and singers use when working on projecting. After taking a deep breath while expanding their bellies, they forcefully expel all the air out on a "ha" sound. Usually, they stand on one side of the theater (or room) and target the opposite side as if they were going to hit it with their "ha" sound. They do this several times until they can feel the deep and rich texture of the projected voice.

You can start practicing this technique in front of a mirror. If after sending the "ha" sound the mirror doesn't get fogged, then it means that you're not breathing from the belly. Once you have mastered the exercise in front of the mirror, you should try it in a room, targeting the opposite wall. While you do this, place both your hands on your belly so that you can feel its rising when you inhale. If the belly doesn't move, then you need to continue practicing until you start breathing correctly. Remember that if you don't breathe from you belly, you cannot project the voice.

Mastering diction

Having good diction involves enunciating and articulating while talking. This implies pronouncing words clearly, making sure that we are understood without ambiguities. A clear diction doesn't mean exaggerating the speech. It is about speaking clearly in a natural fashion, while enunciating and stressing the right syllables and words.

There are several simple exercises actors use when working on their diction. Reading out loud regularly, making sure that you pronounce all words properly, is a good way to improve over time. Another way to improve is by learning soliloquies or poems and reciting them as often as possible, while making an extra effort to enunciate and articulate. The famous Shakespeare's soliloquy "To be or not to be" from *Hamlet*, is often used to practice diction:

> To be, or not to be, that is the question:
> Whether 'tis nobler in the mind to suffer
> The slings and arrows of outrageous fortune,
> Or to take arms against a sea of troubles

And by opposing end them. To die—to sleep,
No more; and by a sleep to say we end
The heart-ache and the thousand natural shocks
That flesh is heir to: 'tis a consummation
Devoutly to be wish'd. To die, to sleep;
To sleep, perchance to dream—ay, there's the rub:
For in that sleep of death what dreams may come,
When we have shuffled off this mortal coil,
Must give us pause—there's the respect
That makes calamity of so long life.
For who would bear the whips and scorns of time,
Th'oppressor's wrong, the proud man's contumely,
The pangs of dispriz'd love, the law's delay,
The insolence of office, and the spurns
That patient merit of th'unworthy takes,
When he himself might his quietus make
With a bare bodkin? Who would fardels bear,
To grunt and sweat under a weary life,
But that the dread of something after death,
The undiscovere'd country, from whose bourn
No traveller returns, puzzles the will,
And makes us rather bear those ills we have
Than fly to others that we know not of?
Thus conscience doth make cowards of us all,
And thus the native hue of resolution
Is sicklied o'er with the pale cast of thought,
And enterprises of great pith and moment
With this regard their currents turn awry
And lose the name of action.

It is also common for actors to repeat tongue twisters several times to warm up the muscles in the mouth before performances. This helps them have optimal diction during the show. There are literally hundreds of tongue twisters available. Three of the most popular ones in the theater are shown below. They have to be learned and repeated several times, each new time faster than the previous one:

Tongue twister 1:
Peter Piper picked a peck of pickled peppers.
A peck of pickled peppers Peter Piper picked.
If Peter Piper picked a peck of pickled peppers,
Where's the peck of pickled peppers Peter Piper picked?

Tongue twister 2:
What a to-do to die today at a minute or two to two,
a thing distinctly hard to say but harder still to do.
For they'll beat a tattoo at a quarter to two: with a rat-ta
tat-tat ta tat-tat ta to-to.
And the dragon will come at the beat of the drum at a
minute or two to two today,
at a minute or two to two.

Tongue twister 3:
You know New York.
You need New York.
You know you need unique New York.

Leaders, like actors, need to warm up and prepare before addressing others. Reading out loud regularly, learning and reciting
poems, or repeating tongue twisters as warm-up exercises can
help them improve their diction.

Conclusion

Leadership presence can be defined as the capacity that leaders
have to be present, in the moment, completely connected to their
own thoughts, able to express their feelings, and very aware of
their surroundings. In order to be more present, leaders can borrow some basic techniques from the theater. They include learning how to breathe from their bellies, adopting a neutral position,
practicing the mirror exercise, and participating in improvisations.

Moreover, leaders, like actors, need to work on mastering
their voices so that they can express their ideas and thoughts with
conviction. This is key in the process of inspiring followers to
pursue and achieve common goals. Mastering the voice implies
being able to control its tones in order to produce variety. It also
involves learning how to project it so that it can be heard. A good
projected voice conveys assurance, control, and respect.

Reflective questions

1. Consider the concept of presence as described by Stella Adler
    and how it applies to leadership in different settings. Reflect
    on leaders you know or have observed in political, corporate,

or community roles. How do they embody the concept of presence, and what impact does it have on their effectiveness?

2. Reflect on your understanding of presence and charisma. Do you believe that presence, unlike charisma, can be learned and developed over time? Think of an example when you could have exhibited a stronger presence in a leadership situation. What do you think you could have done differently to improve your presence in that situation?

3. Reflect on the techniques discussed in the chapter for developing leadership presence (belly breathing, neutral position, mirror exercise, improvisations). Have you or someone you know tried any of these techniques? What was the experience and outcome, and what did it reveal about the process of developing presence?

4. Think about how voice and diction contribute to a leader's presence. Can you recall a leader whose voice and speech mannerisms significantly influence their presence? Reflect on how these elements can be cultivated, and on what their role is in projecting confidence and authority.

5. In the context of digital and remote communication, reflect on the challenges leaders face in maintaining presence. What strategies can be effective in conveying leadership presence through virtual platforms? Consider your own experiences or observations in this area and write or discuss the adaptations necessary for effective virtual leadership presence.

Notes

1 Kissel, H. (2000). *Stella Adler – The Art of Acting: Preface by Marlon Brando compiled & edited by Howard Kissel*. Hal Leonard Corporation (p. 22).

2 THNKR (2012). The speech that made Obama president. Retrieved from https://www.youtube.com/watch?v=OFPwDe22CoY

3 Halpern, B. L. & Lubar, K. (2003). *Leadership Presence*. New York: Gotham Books.

4 Hopper, S. I., Murray, S. L., Ferrara, L. R., & Singleton, J. K. (2019). Effectiveness of diaphragmatic breathing for reducing physiological and psychological stress in adults: A quantitative systematic review. JBI Database of Systematic Reviews and Implementation Reports, 17(9), 1855–1876. https://pubmed.ncbi.nlm.nih.gov/31436595/

5 Spolin, V. (1999). *Improvisation for the Theater* (3rd ed.). Northwestern University Press.

6 Authenticity

Jim Morrison, the talented and charismatic star of the 1960s band
The Doors, understood the essence of authenticity. For Morrison,
true freedom lay in being genuine and true to oneself, rather than
conforming to external expectations or roles. In one of his most
famous quotes, he said:

> The most important kind of freedom is to be what you really
> are. You trade in your reality for a role. You trade in your sense
> for an act. You give up your ability to feel, and in exchange,
> put on a mask. There can't be any large-scale revolution until
> there's a personal revolution, on an individual level. It's got to
> happen inside first.[1]

Morrison's insight is particularly relevant not only for musicians
and actors but especially for leaders, whose job to inspire others
can only be achieved by being authentic. When people don't think
a leader is authentic, there is no inspiration possible. Instead, followers would be cautious of the leaders and would not trust them.

Morrison's perspective on personal revolution being a precur-
sor to larger change is also pertinent to leadership. When a leader
is authentic, they set a powerful example that encourages others to
also be true to themselves. This can lead to a more genuine, committed, and motivated team or community. The authenticity of a
leader can inspire a culture of authenticity within the organization
or group, leading to more meaningful and effective collaboration.

Authentic leadership

Authentic leadership is a relatively new concept in leadership
studies. It originated in the 1990s as a response to an increasing

DOI: 10.4324/9781003349815-8

demand for a more responsible, ethical, and truthful leadership approach. Its emergence is often linked to the many scandals of corruption and mismanagement that have broken in recent years in corporations, banks, and the public sector. Some of the most famous cases include Enron, Lehman Brothers, and Volkswagen, where leaders and managers were intentionally deceiving customers and investors.

The concept of authentic leadership has been defined in various ways. One of the most widespread approaches, proposed by Walumbwa, Avolio et al. (2008),[2] provides a developmental perspective. According to this viewpoint, authentic leadership can be developed and nurtured over time. Defining life events such as career changes, accidents, illnesses, or other unexpected life changes often act as triggers to authentic leadership. Positive psychological capabilities and deep moral values can originate and be developed from those critical life events, which at the same time will foster authentic leadership

Based on this premise, they developed a framework with four elements to define authentic leadership as a pattern of leadership behavior characterized by: (1) a strong self-awareness, (2) a deep moral perspective, (3) a good capacity to process information with balance, and (4) a strong ability to be transparent when working with followers. This pattern of leadership behavior is strongly influenced by both the leader's positive psychological capabilities and by their deep moral values. Each of the four elements plays a crucial role in shaping a leader's authenticity:

1) Strong self-awareness: authentic leaders possess an acute understanding of their personal strengths, weaknesses, values, and motives. This self-awareness is key for leaders to lead with integrity and make decisions aligned with their true self.
2) Deep moral perspective: this element emphasizes a leader's commitment to ethical principles and a strong sense of fairness. It guides them in making decisions that are not only beneficial for their organization but also ethically sound.
3) Balanced processing: this refers to a leader's ability to objectively analyze relevant data before making decisions. It involves considering different viewpoints and avoiding biases, leading to well-rounded and thoughtful decision-making.

4)   Relational transparency: this involves being open and honest in interactions with followers. Authentic leaders are transparent about their thoughts and feelings, which fosters trust and open communication within the team or organization.

These four elements contribute to a leadership style that is not only effective but also deeply rooted in authenticity, helping leaders to earn the respect and trust of their followers.

An important contribution related to this definition of authentic leadership is that it provides clear elements for leaders to consider when they want to develop authentic leadership skills. In this respect, the definition is very useful as it provides a clear theoretical framework that can be used as a foundation to design and implement training programs aimed at developing authentic leadership.

Nevertheless, the framework needs to be supported by further research. Although intuitively we can say that a critical life event is likely to originate and develop strong psychological abilities and moral values, this relation needs to be backed by additional research. Similarly, the link between a deep moral perspective and authentic leadership needs to be explored further.

Discovering our authentic self

Just as an actor delves into the psyche of a character to understand their motivations and backstory, leaders must embark on a journey of self-discovery to uncover their authentic self. This process is more than surface-level introspection; it's about diving into the depths of your personal history, values, and beliefs, much like an actor uncovers the motivations and backstory of their character. This exploration is crucial for leaders as it helps them to connect with who they really are, ensuring their leadership is a reflection of their genuine beliefs and values.

As leaders, we could begin by reflecting on the key moments of our lives that challenged us and changed us. They could be moments of intense joy or sadness. What values were we upholding or struggling with during those times? What did those moments teach us about what is truly important to us? Like an actor seeking to understand the driving forces behind a character, this reflection helps us identify the core values and beliefs that form the foundation of our authentic self.

I often think of the times that challenged me the most and of how I reacted to them. For example, I reflect on how I was able to get back on my feet when my mom passed away, or how I was able to adapt to the career change from banker to professor. By spending time thinking about how I felt, I also reflect on what mattered and did not matter to me when these challenging events happened. This gives me a strong insight into my values. It is important to note that there is a difference between what we say we value versus what our behaviors show we value. For example, I might say that I value social interactions, but when I analyzed a challenging moment, I might find that I tend to isolate myself. Noticing differences like this one when we are reflecting on challenging moments in our lives is key for getting to know ourselves better.

We can also engage in an activity where we list out qualities or adjectives that we feel describe us best. We need to go beyond the surface and delve into why these traits resonate with us. For each trait, we should identify a related core value and write about a life experience (a behavior) where this value was clearly present. This exercise mirrors an actor's method of character development, where deep understanding of personal traits and motivations brings a character to life. For leaders, this activity is essential in bringing their authentic self to the forefront of their leadership style.

Understanding of our authentic self takes time and a lot of introspection. But by thinking of key moments in our lives and analyzing them critically, we can gain strong insights into who we really are. The next step is to work toward embodying these values and beliefs in our leadership, just like an actor who brings authenticity to the characters they portray.

Embodying the authentic self

In simple terms, authenticity in leadership means embracing and expressing one's true self, values, and beliefs. It involves being genuine in interactions, decisions, and leadership style. This authenticity fosters trust and respect from followers and creates an environment where honesty and openness are valued.

But in leadership, as in performance, being authentic is not enough. We have to be able to embody our authenticity, ensuring it resonates with others. This concept is discussed by Donna Ladkin and Steven Taylor in their article, "Enacting the 'true self': Towards a theory of embodied authentic leadership."[3] They argue that while authentic leadership springs from the "true self," its perception by others depends on how this authenticity is embodied.

Thus, authenticity is both the quality of being truthful to oneself and the capacity of embodying the true self in such a way that it can be perceived as truthful by others. The embodiment is crucial. It's about presenting one's true character and values in a way that is transparent and resonates with followers. The use of acting techniques can be instrumental for leaders in this context. These techniques provide leaders with the tools to effectively communicate and express their authentic selves, ensuring that their genuineness is not just felt internally but is also evident and impactful in their leadership style. The capacity to convey authenticity in this dual manner—both internally consistent and externally perceivable—is what sets apart truly authentic leaders from others.

We often define acting as the process of living truthfully under the imaginary circumstances of the play. This definition emphasizes the actor's need to be truthful, to be authentic. There are two acting techniques that can help actors embody authentic emotions so that they can connect their inner selves with the imaginary circumstances of a play. These techniques are Konstantin Stanislavski's "Magic If" and Uta Hagen's "Inner Objects." In the following section, we will discuss these techniques and will relate them to the development of leadership skills.

Stanislavski's "Magic If"

Konstantin Stanislavski revolutionized acting in the early 20th century with his "Method Acting" approach. His techniques represented a departure from the exaggerated styles of the past. It involved actors tapping into their past experiences to elicit genuine emotions and actions. This method gained traction, particularly in the film industry, where nuanced and authentic performances became essential due to the intimacy of close-up shots.

Stanislavski's techniques have since become fundamental in modern acting training globally (Moore, 1960).[4]

Stanislavski's "Magic If" is one of the most important techniques of his acting system. It focuses on aligning an actor's objectives with their character's goals. The technique requires that actors ask themselves what they would do if they were their characters. This technique immerses actors in the play's fictional context by prompting them to contemplate their reactions in the character's situation. Stanislavski stresses that actors have to imagine their actions in the character's shoes. The key question actors explore during role preparation is, "What would I do if I were this character in these specific circumstances?" (Stanislavski, 1988).[5]

The "Magic If" technique allows actors to produce genuine emotions that originate from actions they have adopted as if they were the characters. They are not faking anything. They are acting as if they were their characters in their characters' circumstances, which produces the genuine emotions.

A few years ago, I had the opportunity to play Agoracritus from Aristophanes' *The Knights* at Theatro Technics, a theater company in London. This is a character that evolves from a simple sausage-seller at the beginning of the play, to a political leader at the end. Agoracritus, despite the play's satirical tone, needed to evolve authentically into a persuasive politician, capable of influencing the masses through his speeches (Aristophanes, 424 BCE/2003).[6] This transition from a comedic character to a credible political figure was a key element in convincing both the characters within the play and the audience of my transformation.

My approach to embodying Agoracritus, despite having no personal experience in political leadership, was grounded in Stanislavski's "Magic If." I imagined myself in Agoracritus's shoes, especially during his pivotal speeches. I drew parallels between his situation and my own experiences teaching in large university lectures. By reflecting on my feelings and behaviors in these teaching scenarios, I could authentically replicate similar emotions and actions for Agoracritus. This process allowed me to deeply connect with the character's experiences, enhancing my performance and making it more relatable and genuine for the audience.

In the context of authentic leadership, Stanislavski's "Magic If" can be an effective tool for leaders seeking to exhibit authentic behaviors and cultivate genuine connections within their teams and organizations. When we employ the "Magic If," we delve into hypothetical scenarios where we imagine ourselves in the shoes of our team members or in different leadership situations. This imaginative exercise is not about pretending or faking emotions; rather, it's about exploring genuine responses to imagined circumstances. By asking, "What would I do if I were faced with this challenge?" or "How would I react if I were in this team member's position?," we, as leaders, can uncover authentic reactions and insights that stem from our own values and experiences.

In addition, the "Magic If" approach helps in building empathy, a crucial component of leadership. Understanding the perspectives and feelings of team members enables leaders to respond in ways that are not only effective but also human. It also fosters a culture of trust and openness, as team members feel genuinely understood and valued.

Furthermore, the "Magic If" can aid leaders in aligning their actions with their core values and beliefs. By constantly reflecting on how their decisions align with their authentic selves in various scenarios, leaders can maintain integrity and consistency in their leadership style. This alignment is key in building credibility and trust among team members.

Leaders can also use the "Magic If" in vision-setting and embodying the values of the organization. Imagining how they would act and communicate in a future where the organization's goals and values are fully realized can help leaders to more authentically embody and promote these ideals in the present.

Incorporating the "Magic If" into leadership practices offers a path to authentic leadership. It allows leaders to explore and express genuine emotions and reactions, build empathy with their team, and ensure their actions are consistently aligned with their values. This approach not only enhances the leader's authenticity but also fosters a more authentic and cohesive team environment.

Hagen's inner objects

Uta Hagen's method involving "inner objects" centers around the use of specific, personal images to evoke the necessary emotions and physical responses for a role. Actors employ this technique to connect with their character's fictional circumstances. They do so by recalling vivid, personal memories at precise moments of the play to elicit specific emotional and physiological reactions. This process, as outlined by Hagen (1991),[7] requires repeated practice to ensure these reactions become almost automatic on stage.

The process to identify effective inner objects is a complex one. Actors must experiment with various memories to discover which ones trigger the right emotions and reactions. A typical method involves sitting quietly, eyes closed, in a relaxed state, and mentally going through personal experiences to find those that resonate with the character's emotional state.

Consider, for instance, a scene requiring an actor to portray fear. The actor would need to recall a personal experience that genuinely frightened them. If I were the actor, a powerful memory for me could be when I encountered a snake in my childhood home in Venezuela. During visualization, I would need to immerse myself in the details of that moment: the time of day, the room's ambiance, colors, textures, smells, and sounds. I would concentrate on these details and observe my emotional response.

To test this technique, I actually sat in my bedroom, closed my eyes, relaxed, and then started remembering the snake incident. I mentally revisited every aspect of the moment when I saw the snake: the room's layout, the smell, how hot it was, the color of the walls, the furniture, etc. Unfortunately, no fear emerged. I continued exploring the moment and imagined myself walking around the room while looking at the snake. I started touching the walls, the furniture, feeling the temperature of the objects in the room, and suddenly, as I was touching a purple velvet pillow under my hand—I finally experienced a surge of fear. This discovery was crucial: it wasn't the visual memory of the snake that triggered fear, but the tactile sensation of the velvet pillow. The sensation of touching that pillow became the inner object that I would need to recall to convincingly portray fear in a performance. Repeatedly evoking this tactile sensation in rehearsals would help condition my response in performance, a concept known in acting as "sense memory."

Authentic leadership is rooted in being true to oneself, understanding one's values, and expressing genuine emotions. By using Hagen's approach, leaders can connect more profoundly with their own experiences, allowing them to lead from a place of sincerity and self-awareness. This involves identifying memories or experiences that evoke strong, genuine emotions and using them as a reference point in leadership scenarios.

When setting goals or driving change, leaders can use this technique to anchor their vision in their own authentic experiences. By recalling moments of inspiration or triumph, leaders can communicate their vision with genuine passion and conviction. This not only makes the vision more compelling but also demonstrates the leader's true commitment and belief in the direction they are advocating.

Moreover, in times of decision-making, leaders can utilize "inner objects" to align their choices with their authentic selves. By reflecting on past experiences that shaped their values and principles, leaders can ensure their decisions are a true reflection of who they are. This consistency between actions and values is a hallmark of authentic leadership.

Similarly, when a leader has a hard time connecting with a challenging situation facing their team or company, the leader might recall a personal moment of struggle or vulnerability in order to make a stronger connection with the adverse circumstances. Reliving the emotions and physical sensations of that experience enables the leader to genuinely understand and relate to the challenging situation. This connection is not contrived but stems from a real place within the leader, enhancing the authenticity of the interaction.

Adapting Hagen's "inner objects" technique in leadership practices can profoundly impact the authenticity of a leader. It allows for genuine emotional connections, decisions that reflect true values, and communication that resonates deeply with others. This approach not only builds trust and respect within the team but also establishes the leader as genuinely connected and empathetic.

Conclusion

In this chapter, we have explored the concept of authenticity in leadership through the lens of acting techniques—specifically, Konstantin Stanislavski's "Magic If" and Uta Hagen's "Inner Objects." These methods, though originally intended for actors, offer useful insights into the development and expression of authentic leadership.

Authentic leadership, as we have seen, is about more than just being true to oneself. It involves a deep understanding of one's values, experiences, and emotions, and the ability to convey this authenticity in a manner that resonates with and inspires others. Stanislavski's "Magic If" encourages leaders to use their imagination and connect with the different roles they have to play as leaders. It also helps them put themselves in the shoes of others, fostering empathy and a genuine connection. Similarly, Hagen's technique of "Inner Objects" allows leaders to tap into their personal reservoir of experiences, using these memories to anchor their decisions and leadership styles.

Reflective questions

1. Think back to when you first assumed a leadership role. How have your personal experiences since then shaped your approach to leadership? Reflect on how these experiences have influenced your authenticity as a leader.
2. Recall a situation where you faced an ethical dilemma in your role as a leader. How did you navigate this, and what did the process reveal about your core values and authentic leadership style?
3. Consider a recent interaction with a team member who was facing a problem. How could you have applied the "Magic If" technique to better understand their situation? Reflect on how this might have changed your response or approach.
4. Reflect on an occasion where your authentic leadership style seemed at odds with your organization's culture. How did you reconcile this conflict, and what did you learn about maintaining authenticity in diverse environments?
5. Think about a time when you had to significantly adapt your leadership approach to suit a new team or project. How did you ensure that you remained true to your core values and authentic self during this adaptation?

Notes

1 James, L. (1981). Jim Morrison: Ten years gone. *Creem Magazine*. Retrieved from https://archives.waiting-forthe-sun.net/Pages/Interviews/JimInterviews/TenYearsGone.html

2 Walumbwa, F. O., Avolio, B. J., Gardner, W. L., Wernsing, T. S., and Peterson S. J. (2008). Authentic leadership: Development and validation of a theory-based measure. *Journal of Management*, 34(1), 89–126.
3 Ladkin, D., & Taylor, S. S. (2010). Enacting the "true self": Towards a theory of embodied authentic leadership. *The Leadership Quarterly*, 64–74.
4 Moore, S. (1960). *The Stanislavski System*. New York: Penguin Books.
5 Stanislavski, C. (1988). *An Actor Prepares*. London: Methuen.
6 Aristophanes (2003). *The Birds and Other Plays: The Knights* (D. Berrett & A. Summerstein, Trans). London: Penguin. (Original work published 424 BCE).
7 Hagen, U. (1991). *A Challenge for the Actor*. New York: Scribner.

7   Communication

Communication involves an interplay of verbal and non-verbal messages. This interaction is reminiscent of the art of acting, where performers must master the subtleties of conveying emotions and intentions (the subtext) without relying solely on dialogue (the text). The unspoken often conveys more than the spoken word. For example, in a scenario where a person greets another with a smile and a nod, no words are exchanged, yet a warm welcome is clearly communicated, showing how non-verbal cues can effectively convey sentiments and intentions.

Antoine de Saint-Exupéry, the French writer, poet, and pioneering aviator, captures the complex nature of human communication in this quote from his famous book *The Little Prince* (*Le Petit Prince*): "I shall look at you out of the corner of my eye, and you will say nothing. Words are the source of misunderstandings."[1] This quote elegantly underscores the intricate and often misunderstood dynamics of human interaction, where what is left unsaid can be just as impactful, if not more so, than the words we choose to vocalize.

This chapter explores the world of leadership communication by looking at both non-linguistic and linguistic elements. It connects them with acting techniques, providing leaders with invaluable tools to refine their persuasive skills and enhance their communication abilities. From a non-linguistic point of view, the chapter will cover elements related to body language, facial expressions, and physical movement, among others. From a linguistic perspective, it will review key concepts from the field of rhetoric and will establish their relevance in leadership communication. These concepts include the role of character (ethos), emotions (pathos), and reason (logos) in persuasive acts. Finally, the chapter will cover storytelling as a key tool in leadership communication. People often remember

DOI: 10.4324/9781003349815-9

stories long after they've forgotten raw data or facts. Stories have the unique ability to captivate an audience, evoke emotions, and convey complex ideas in a memorable and relatable manner.

Communication

Communication can be defined as the process of exchanging information, ideas, thoughts, feelings, and emotions through various means such as speech, writing, gestures, visual aids, etc. It plays a fundamental role in human interaction and is essential for conveying messages, building relationships, and facilitating understanding among individuals and groups. The process of communication is often defined in terms of four elements: sender, receiver, message, and noise.

The sender is the person or entity who initiates the communication by encoding a message. They are responsible for formulating and transmitting the information to the intended receiver. On the other hand, the receiver is the individual or group for whom the message is intended. The receiver decodes and interprets the message to understand its meaning.

The message is the information, idea, or content that the sender wishes to convey to the receiver. It can take various forms, such as spoken words, written text, visual images, or non-verbal cues. Finally, noise refers to any interference or factors that can disrupt or distort the communication process. It can be internal (psychological or physiological distractions) or external (environmental factors, competing messages) and may hinder the accurate transmission and reception of the message.

In the world of acting, the importance of effective communication is at the heart of the craft. Actors rely on their ability to convey a character's thoughts, emotions, and intentions to the audience with precision and authenticity. The parallels between the principles of communication and acting are striking. Just as the sender in communication encodes a message to reach the receiver, an actor must skillfully convey the character's lines, emotions, and motivations to the audience. The receiver in communication, much like the audience in the theater, plays a vital role in decoding and interpreting the message or performance to grasp its intended meaning.

Moreover, the message itself, whether it is a scripted dialogue, a monologue, or a silent expression, is the actor's way of connecting with the audience and evoking emotions. Just as in communication, where the message can take various forms, actors utilize a diverse range of tools, from spoken words to physical gestures. Additionally, noise in acting can come in various forms, such as distractions on the set, technical difficulties, or even the actor's own inner turmoil. These distractions may interfere with the actor's ability to deliver a convincing performance, much like noise can disrupt the communication process. By recognizing and mitigating these distractions, actors, like effective communicators, aim to ensure that their message is received and understood as intended. When developing leadership skills through acting techniques, understanding the parallels between communication and acting can be a powerful tool in mastering the art of conveying messages, building relationships, and fostering understanding among individuals and groups.

A historical overview of leadership communication

The birth of democracy is often considered the beginning of the study of leadership from a communication perspective. We can trace the evolution of rhetoric from the Greco-Roman period until the 20th century. In ancient Greece, the birth of democracy in approximately 460 BCE resulted in the need for new leadership skills. As young male citizens were given the opportunity to participate in the political life of the city, the teaching of rhetoric, broadly defined as the art of persuasion, emerged as a key element in the training of future Athenian leaders.[2]

Itinerant teachers of rhetoric, known as sophists, became quite popular. In addition to persuasion, they taught future leaders how to live well in Athens. While Plato adopted an anti-rhetoric position, considering it a set of tricks aimed at deceiving an audience, Aristotle thought that the use of persuasive language was an effective tool to demonstrate the truth.

During the Roman period, rhetoric became central in the preparation of citizens for public life. Its connection with leadership and power was evident. It was not only perceived as essential for a successful professional life but also for a personal one. Moreover, it was thought of as a discipline requiring a strong sense of responsibility and ethics. Cicero's *De Oratore* (*On the Orator*)[3] is considered one of the most representative rhetorical treaties of the Roman period.

In the medieval period, the importance of oral communication was evidenced by the appearance of various treatises devoted to sermons. Saint Augustine, who emerged as a key figure between the Greco-Roman period and the Middle Ages, used rhetoric to defend and spread Christianity. He also backed the teaching of rhetoric in Christian education so that the Church would have powerful advocates.

From the 14th to the 17th centuries, prominent humanist intellectuals including Petrarch and Valla argued that rhetoric was a much more important discipline than philosophy. After the invention of the printing press in the 15th century, rhetoric began to be linked to the printed media, and its study started to be associated with a good education. It was during the Renaissance that the study of rhetoric reached its greatest importance.

During the 18th and 19th centuries, thinkers of the Enlightenment influenced by science and rational thinking started to question the power of language. As a result, rhetoric began to lose its relevance. Nevertheless, writers of the Scottish Enlightenment such as Blaire, Campbell, and Kames kept emphasizing the importance of rhetoric in education, and continued exploring topics from the Greco-Roman tradition such as style, argumentation, and ways to achieve personal refinement.

In the 20th century, with the surge of radio and television, the focus of leadership communication, mainly in politics, shifted from print to mass media. Oratory and persuasion skills became key in allowing political leaders to share visions, communicate plans, and amass support. Seminal political speeches such as Winston Churchill's "This was their finest hour" in 1940 and Martin Luther King Jr.'s "I have a dream" in 1963 changed history after being broadcast on radio and TV respectively.

More recently, with the emergence of digital technology and social media, the way leaders communicate continues to evolve. It is common for political and business leaders, among others, to often use online comments, blogs, or videos in order to share their visions and strategies with followers. Their posts are shared with large groups of followers and stakeholders through social media.

Developing non-verbal leadership communication through acting

In leadership, just like in the theater, non-verbal elements often carry more weight than the words we use. Just like actors, leaders rely on body language, facial expressions, and physical movements to convey emotions and intentions, leaders can tap into these non-verbal cues to become better at connecting with and influencing others. Acting techniques can be a valuable resource for honing these non-verbal communication skills.

Body language

Effective body language is not only about posture and gestures; it also emanates from within. Just as actors tap into their characters' emotions to portray them authentically, leaders can harness their inner emotions to convey sincerity and connection through their body language. Leaders should strive to align their inner emotions with their outward expressions. When their body language authentically mirrors their feelings, it fosters trust and credibility. Exercising presence, as seen in Chapter 5, allows leaders to connect on a deeper level. Being mindful of one's own emotions and reactions can enhance the authenticity of body language.

A good exercise, drawn from the world of acting, targets the enhancement of your body language. Here's a step-by-step approach. Before a significant meeting or interaction, take a brief moment to reflect on your emotions and intentions. Pay attention to how you genuinely feel about the subject matter or the individuals you'll be engaging with. Try to identify your authentic emotions. It's important to acknowledge that as a leader, you may encounter a range of emotions, including negative ones like anxiety, frustration, or apprehension. Accept these feelings without judgment; they are a natural part of being human.

As you engage in the interaction, focus on being mindful of your emotional state. Notice how your body responds to these emotions. You might observe tension in your shoulders, a faster heartbeat, or changes in your breathing patterns. If you find yourself experiencing strong negative emotions during the interaction, practice self-regulation techniques. These may include deep breathing exercises, counting to ten silently, or briefly excusing yourself to regain composure.

While it's essential to be authentic, leaders can adapt their body language to convey emotions appropriately. For instance, if you're feeling anxious, you can maintain eye contact, use reassuring gestures, and adopt a calm posture to help ease the tension in the room. Keep in mind that this exercise is a skill that improves with practice. Over time, you'll become more proficient at recognizing and managing your emotions, allowing you to convey authenticity and composure through your body language. For more in-depth guidance on emotional intelligence and further techniques for regulating emotions, you can refer to Chapter 8.

Here a good exercise inspired by acting to target body language is this one. Before an important meeting or interaction, take a moment to reflect on your emotions and intentions. Identify how you genuinely feel about the subject or the people involved. As you engage in the interaction, let your body language naturally reflect these emotions. This exercise encourages leaders to connect with their inner emotional landscape and convey authenticity through their body language. You will probably find some emotions that you'll need to regulate. That's normal. For more on emotional intelligence, and regulating emotions, see Chapter 8.

Facial expressions

Actors are taught that for a facial expression to be believable, it has to come from within. Effective facial expressions are an immediate reflection of one's emotions. Leaders can enhance their non-verbal communication by being in touch with their feelings and using their facial expressions to convey sincerity. Forcing facial expressions has the potential to be perceived as fake and unauthentic.

Authentic facial expressions that align with inner emotions can help leaders connect with their team members on a personal level. When leaders genuinely show empathy or enthusiasm, it fosters emotional resonance. Being aware of and responsive to the emotions of others is vital in leadership. Leaders can use their facial expressions to convey empathy and understanding. Chapter 8 discusses emotional intelligence and leadership in detail.

Regularly take a moment to check in with your own emotions. You could use a mirror to observe your facial expressions as you recall a recent experience that evoked strong feelings. Practice recognizing and authentically displaying these emotions through your facial expressions. This exercise helps leaders become more in tune with their emotions and enhances their ability to convey empathy and sincerity.

Physical movements

Physical movements are powerful tools for communicating determination and confidence. Leaders can benefit from acting techniques that help align their movements with their inner state, thereby enhancing their non-verbal communication. By understanding the power of purposeful physical movements, leaders can project authority and assurance.

In acting, performers are taught not to move on stage without a clear reason. Every movement must have a purpose tied to their character's objectives and intentions. Actors delve into the "why" behind each movement, asking questions like, "Where is my character going, and why?" This deep understanding allows actors to infuse their actions with meaning and authenticity, effectively conveying their character's emotions and intentions to captivate the audience and create a compelling performance.

This lesson holds valuable insights for leaders as well. By applying this concept to their non-verbal communication, leaders can ensure that every physical action serves a purpose and effectively communicates their intentions. Movement can be a strategic tool to engage an audience or team members and underscore key points. For instance, leaders can practice walking and gesturing in a manner that resonates with their inner intentions and emotions. As they move, they should be mindful of their internal state and how it influences their physical actions. The goal is to make movements an authentic expression of their thoughts and feelings.

When individuals move without a clear destination or purpose, whether on stage or in an office setting, they often appear nervous or uncertain. Aimless pacing or fidgeting can convey insecurity and distract from the message being communicated. By contrast, leaders who apply the principles of purposeful movement project a sense of direction, confidence, and purpose, which can inspire trust and respect among their audience or team members. Understanding the impact of purposeless movement reinforces the importance of aligning physical actions with intentions in effective non-verbal communication.

Developing verbal leadership communication through acting

On Rhetoric[4] by Aristotle stands as the cornerstone in the study of persuasive communication and the art of influence. This text has provided invaluable insights into the power of effective rhetoric for over two millennia. It focuses on how individuals can use language, argumentation, and persuasion to sway others and achieve their objectives. Aristotle delves into the intricacies of effective communication, emphasizing the importance of ethos (credibility), pathos (emotional appeal), and logos (logical reasoning) as essential elements in convincing an audience. We will use these three elements, also called Aristotle's artistic proofs, as framework for discussing verbal leadership communication.

Ethos (character and credibility)

Ethos, the first of Aristotle's artistic proofs, revolves around the credibility and character of the speaker. Aristotle argued that for a message to be persuasive, the speaker must establish themselves as a trustworthy and authoritative source. This involves not only expertise in the subject matter but also a demonstration of integrity and sincerity. Ethos is about building trust and credibility with the audience. When individuals perceive a speaker as knowledgeable, honest, and virtuous, they are more inclined to be persuaded by the speaker's message.

Building credibility is a gradual process that requires a deep understanding of one's values and beliefs. Making a list of what truly matters to you, as we discussed in Chapter 4, helps you align your words and actions with your fundamental principles. This list creates a solid foundation of trustworthiness and authority for communicating ethos. The alignment resembles what actors do when they immerse themselves in a character. They must comprehend the character's values and beliefs to deliver a convincing performance.

Just as actors carefully embrace the appearance and behavior of their characters to immerse the audience in the story, leaders must present themselves in a manner that aligns with their intended message and role. This alignment enhances their credibility among followers. However, this process involves more than merely "dressing the part." It also encompasses speaking appropriately, adopting the right body language, and maintaining an overall conduct that fits their leadership role. For instance, a CEO must look like a CEO, move like a CEO, and talk like a CEO if they want to improve their credibility.

Choosing the right medium is another aspect of ethos. Just as actors choose the right stage and setting for their performance to lend authenticity to their roles, leaders should select the appropriate platform and context for their message. This ensures that their message is conveyed in a manner that enhances their credibility. A famous experiment involving American violinist Joshua Bell provides a compelling illustration of the importance of context and medium in building ethos.[5] In this experiment, Bell, one of the world's most renowned musicians, played the violin in a Washington, D.C., metro station during morning rush hour. Bell's performance, which would typically command high ticket prices in sold-out concert halls, went virtually unnoticed by the busy commuters.

The significance of this experiment lies in its demonstration that even an extraordinary talent like Bell, when placed in an incongruent context, can fail to capture the attention and appreciation of the audience. In the bustling and mundane environment of a metro station, Bell's virtuosity was overshadowed by the surrounding distractions. For leaders, this experiment serves as a reminder that the choice of medium and context can significantly impact how their message is received and the credibility they project. Just as Bell's performance needed the right setting and audience to be truly appreciated, leaders must carefully consider where and how they deliver their messages to maximize their persuasive impact.

Lastly, just as actors need the right audience to appreciate their performance, leaders must consider their target audience. Tailoring their communication style and message to resonate with their audience's values, interests, and expectations can significantly bolster their ethos. When leaders effectively "dress the part," choose the right medium, and connect with their audience, they enhance their credibility, making their message more persuasive and influential.

Pathos (emotional appeal)

Pathos, the second artistic proof, deals with the emotional appeal of a message. Aristotle recognized that humans are not purely rational beings but are deeply influenced by their emotions. Therefore, effective communication should aim to evoke genuine emotions in the audience.

In the theater, eliciting emotions is a core objective. Actors endeavor to make the audience feel joy, sadness, anger, or empathy, depending on the storyline. In the same way, leaders can harness the power of pathos by connecting with their own emotions and using them to engage and inspire their team or audience.

As seen in Chapter 6 on authenticity, the "Magic If" technique can help leaders elicit genuine emotions. This technique involves asking yourself the question, "What would I do if I were the character in this situation?" It's a way for actors to connect with their characters on an emotional and psychological level, helping them understand and portray the character's motivations, thoughts, and actions more authentically. By using the "Magic If," actors imagine themselves in the character's circumstances, considering how they would react based on their character's background, desires, and relationships. This technique allows actors to tap into their own emotions and experiences while staying true to the character's unique perspective.

Logos (logical and rational appeal)

The third artistic proof, logos, pertains to the logical and rational aspects of communication. Aristotle emphasized the importance of presenting arguments and ideas in a clear, structured, and coherent manner. For a message to be persuasive, it must be supported by sound reasoning and evidence.

In acting, a well-structured narrative is essential for the audience to follow and understand the story. While playwrights primarily shape the narrative, actors play a crucial role in conveying the story's logic through their performance. Much like leaders who need to present their ideas coherently, actors must ensure that their portrayal of a character aligns with the overarching narrative.

One useful exercise for leaders, inspired by acting techniques, is to analyze courtroom scenes from movies or TV shows. These scenes often feature lawyers presenting logical arguments, supporting evidence, and engaging in persuasive dialogue. Leaders can observe how lawyers use logic and reasoning to make their case and convince a jury or judge. This exercise can help leaders understand how to structure their own arguments effectively and present their ideas with clarity and persuasion.

Additionally, leaders can borrow from actors' techniques for memorizing lines and staying organized in their delivery. Similar to actors, who often integrate physical movements and actions into their rehearsals to reinforce their memory of complex scripts, leaders can adopt a comparable approach when preparing for critical presentations or discussions. By associating specific movements or gestures with key points or arguments in their content, leaders create a powerful memory aid. This technique ensures that their logical arguments are not only remembered but also delivered convincingly and coherently during their communication. As a result, leaders can significantly enhance their overall effectiveness in conveying their messages to their audience.

Incorporating elements of logical and rational appeal into their communication, leaders can enhance their ability to persuade and influence others effectively. Just as actors contribute to the narrative's clarity on stage, leaders who master the art of logos can guide their audience through complex ideas and arguments, making their messages more compelling and impactful.

Storytelling

Storytelling is a timeless art. Humans have been telling stories for centuries. Stories exist in all cultures. As children, we are told stories by our parents or guardians. Stories have the potential to captivate and inspire. They stimulate our imagination and make us dream. Just as actors convey a character's journey and emotions through a well-scripted narrative, leaders can harness the power of storytelling to engage their audience on a personal and emotional level. Stories have a unique ability to connect with people, evoke empathy, and convey complex ideas in a memorable and relatable manner.

Leaders can use storytelling to illustrate their points, provide context, and make their messages more accessible. A well-told story can inspire, motivate, and instill values in others. When leaders share personal or relatable anecdotes, they humanize themselves, making them more approachable and relatable to their team members or followers. Storytelling also helps create a shared sense of purpose and vision, aligning individuals with a common narrative.

Incorporating storytelling into leadership communication doesn't require elaborate scripts or theatrical performances. Instead, leaders can focus on crafting narratives that resonate with their audience, highlighting key lessons, challenges, and successes. By weaving stories into their messages, leaders can enhance their ability to connect with others, inspire action, and leave a lasting impact.

One technique that leaders could use to become better at storytelling is graphic vividness. Actors often use it for its ability to captivate and engage audiences. Graphic vividness refers to the quality of being highly detailed, descriptive, and visually evocative when telling a story. It involves seeing the images of what we are telling so that others can see them too. When actors employ graphic vividness, they visualize every detail with such clarity that it becomes almost tangible. This immersive approach goes beyond mere words; it evokes sensory experiences and emotions that resonate deeply with the audience.

For actors, seeing and feeling what they convey is essential because it ensures that the audience sees and feels it too. If the actor sees what they are talking about, the audience sees it. If the actor feels it, the audience feels it. When actors utilize words and descriptions that paint a vivid mental picture for themselves, this mental imagery is seamlessly transferred to the audience. As a result, the storytelling becomes a shared experience that is not only engaging but also memorable and impactful. By stimulating their own imagination and adopting this technique, leaders can craft compelling and unforgettable narratives for their audience.

One notable advocate of storytelling in leadership is Indra Nooyi, former chairman and CEO of PepsiCo. In her Five Cs model of leadership (competency, courage and confidence, communication, consistency, and compass), she gives communication a special place. When she recounted her experience at the Seventh Annual BlogHer Conference in San Diego in 2011, she shared a personal story about her communication journey:

> When I first came to the United States, I used to debate, and I used to be on debating teams. But I used to speak so fast because culturally, I grew up in an environment where people speak very fast. Fortunately, Yale had a requirement that unless you pass the communications course, you couldn't graduate from the first year to the second year in business school. I flunked the first time I took the communications course. So over the summer, I took it again, which was the best thing that happened because I learned to sync my brain with my output from my mouth, so I started to slow down what I was saying. Huge difference. So, I encourage all of you to invest in communication skills; it's critically important.[6]

Nooyi's personal story highlights the transformative impact of refining one's communication skills. It serves as a reminder that even leaders with remarkable abilities can enhance their effectiveness by mastering the art of storytelling and communication. Just as Nooyi's journey at Yale transformed her communication style and made her a more impactful leader, leaders can also harness the power of storytelling to connect with their audience, inspire action, and drive their messages home.

Conclusion

This chapter focused on leadership communication. It explored the evolution of communication and its connection with acting techniques to enhance both non-verbal and verbal communication skills. The chapter introduced Aristotle's persuasive principles—credibility (ethos), emotional appeal (pathos), and logical reasoning (logos)—as foundational elements for effective leadership communication. In addition, the chapter highlighted the importance of storytelling as a way to engage and inspire in leadership contexts. The concept of graphic vividness, borrowed from acting, was discussed as a means to create compelling and memorable narratives. Finally, Indra Nooyi's example served to illustrate how refining communication skills can transform a leader's effectiveness, highlighting the importance of continuous improvement.

Reflective questions

1. Think about how you currently use non-verbal communication, such as body language and facial expressions, in your leadership role, and how you can improve these aspects to enhance your leadership presence.
2. Think of a recent leadership communication challenge you encountered. How did your approach align with the principles of ethos, pathos, and logos? What adjustments could you make in similar situations in the future?
3. Can you recall a specific instance in your career where storytelling played a crucial role in conveying a message or inspiring action? What emotions or reactions did it evoke, and what made the story memorable?
4. Reflect on your current storytelling style. In what ways can you incorporate the technique of graphic vividness, as discussed in this chapter, to make your narratives more compelling and impactful?
5. How can you apply the insights from this chapter to foster a culture of effective communication within your organization, whether in your current role or in a future leadership position? What steps can you take to ensure that your colleagues or team members feel heard, understood, and motivated by your communication style and approach?

Notes

1 Saint-Exupéry, A. d. (2000). *The Little Prince* (R. Howard, Trans., p. 60). Mariner Books Houghton Mifflin Harcourt. (Original work published 1943.)
2 Jackson, B. & Parry, K. (2011). *A Very Short, Fairly Interesting, and Reasonably Cheap Book about Studying Leadership*. Second edition, London: Sage.

3 Cicero (1976). *De oratore* (E. W. Sutton & H. Rackham, Trans.). Cambridge, MA: Loeb Classical Library.
4 Aristotle (1991). *On Rhetoric: A Theory of Civic Discourse* (G. A. Kennedy, Trans.). New York/Oxford: Oxford University Press.
5 Weingarten, G. (2014, October 14). Setting the record straight on the Joshua Bell experiment. *The Washington Post*. Retrieved from https:// www.washingtonpost.com/news/style/wp/2014/10/14/gene-weingarten-setting-the-record-straight-on-the-joshua-bell-experiment/
6 Nooyi, Indra (2011). Five Cs of Leadership. https://www.youtube .com/watch?v=u0DMaydBOxk (accessed on 25 January 2024).

8 Emotional intelligence

For the American poet Maya Angelou, empathy was a universal trait. "I think we all have empathy. We may not have enough courage to display it,"[1] she said in a *New York Times* interview that took place shortly before her passing in 2014. She was talking about Kofi Annan, the UN Secretary General and Nobel Peace Prize laureate. Angelou thought Annan had a profound capacity to understand and connect with others. But likewise, she thought that all human beings have the capacity to empathize.

Building upon Angelou's perspective, this chapter explores the notion that emotional intelligence in general, and empathy in particular, are essential traits that can be cultivated and developed. We can become more empathetic if we work on it. This is where acting comes in handy, because the main job of actors is to put themselves in the shoes of their characters. Emotional intelligence and empathy are at the heart of what it is to be an actor.

But what is empathy? Empathy is the ability to grasp and personally share the emotions of another person. It encompasses two essential dimensions: the cognitive aspect, which involves understanding someone else's feelings, and the affective aspect, where one actually experiences what the other person is feeling. Empathy goes beyond mere sympathy, as it requires not only comprehension but also a capacity to connect with others' emotions, demonstrating sensitivity and compassion.[2]

In a world dominated by individual interests and money, empathy has become a rare commodity, especially among leaders. In this context, Angelou's praise of Anan's empathetic skills seems particularly significant. Shortages of empathy are more prevalent than ever, especially in politics and business where leaders rarely show altruism or compassion for others.[3]

DOI: 10.4324/9781003349815-10

The 2021 incident involving Vishal Garg, CEO of Better.co m,[4] exemplifies the growing concern about the lack of empathy in leadership. When Garg abruptly fired 900 employees over a Zoom call, it highlighted a disregard for the impact of such actions on individuals' lives. This approach, especially before the holiday season, lacked the sensitivity and personal touch expected in handling such significant career and life-altering decisions. This case serves as a reminder of the importance of empathy in leadership roles, where the human element should be at the forefront of all decision-making processes, particularly in times of crisis or change.

Emotional intelligence

Emotional intelligence, in simple terms, refers to a person's capacity to understand and effectively manage their own emotions as well as the emotions of others. The concept is often abbreviated as EQ, which stands for emotional quotient. EQ has become increasingly significant in leadership studies, in which it is considered a crucial component of effective leadership and interpersonal relationships (Goleman, 1995; Mayer & Salovey, 1997).

The four core components of emotional intelligence are self-awareness, self-regulation, social awareness, and relationship management (Mayer & Salovey, 1997). Daniel Goleman, who has popularized the concept in recent years, builds on these core components and defines five core components of emotional intelligence within a leadership context: self-awareness, self-regulation, motivation, empathy, and social skills (Goleman, 1998). We will use Goleman's five components as a framework for discussion in this chapter.

Self-awareness

Self-awareness is the foundation of emotional intelligence and involves recognizing and understanding your own emotions, strengths, weaknesses, values, and how your emotions impact your behavior and decisions. It sets the stage for improving the other four aspects of emotional intelligence. Leaders who are self-aware tend to be confident and open to constructive feedback. Chapter 4 of this book discusses self-awareness in detail.

A leader who is self-aware is able to take steps to manage their anxiety, anger, or sadness effectively, leading to better decision-making and more constructive interactions with their team and colleagues. For instance, imagine a manager who is aware of their tendency to become anxious when facing tight deadlines. This self-awareness enables them to implement stress-reduction techniques, delegate tasks more effectively, and communicate openly with their team about any challenges they may encounter. By managing their anxiety, the manager can maintain a positive work environment and lead their team through challenging situations with resilience and composure.

Self-regulation

Self-regulation is the ability to manage and control your emotional responses and impulses. It involves staying calm under pressure, adapting to change, and avoiding impulsive reactions. Self-regulation enables individuals to think before they act and make rational decisions even in emotionally charged situations. Leaders who can self-regulate their emotions tend to be comfortable with ambiguity and change. They are also trusted by their teams for their capacity to deal with adversity in a calm way.

Imagine a healthcare professional, the chief of the emergency department, who faces a high-stress situation in the emergency room. If they have strong self-regulation skills, they would be able to maintain composure, prioritize patient care, and make critical decisions calmly. Their response to the critical situation would set an example for their teams. Their ability to regulate their emotions would ensure that they provide the best care possible for the patient, even in intense circumstances.

Motivation

Motivation in the context of emotional intelligence refers to the ability to set and pursue goals with enthusiasm and persistence, even in the face of challenges and setbacks. It involves a deep passion for achieving personal and professional objectives.

Leaders who are motivated in this sense tend to be passionate and optimistic.

Let's consider the case of a dedicated project manager, Sarah, who exemplifies motivation in the workplace. She is tasked with leading a cross-functional team to develop and launch a new software product for her company. This project is critical for the company's growth and success in a highly competitive market. Sarah is deeply passionate about delivering a top-notch product. She believes in the value it will bring to the customers and the company. This passion fuels her commitment to excellence, pushing her to go the extra mile in every aspect of the project.

During the project's execution, the team encounters unexpected technical issues, delays, and resource constraints. However, Sarah remains persistent in her pursuit of the project's objectives. She motivates the team to overcome these challenges by emphasizing the long-term benefits of their work. Sarah maintains a positive attitude even when confronted with setbacks. She communicates her optimism to the team, focusing on solutions rather than dwelling on problems. This positivity not only keeps team morale high but also fosters a can-do spirit among her colleagues.

Empathy

Empathy, as previously discussed, is a central element of emotional intelligence. It entails the capacity to recognize and understand the emotions, needs, and perspectives of others. Empathetic individuals can connect with people on a deeper level, which is invaluable in leadership roles, where building relationships and understanding team dynamics are crucial.

Let's take the example of an employee who expresses frustration to their manager due to a heavy workload. Instead of dismissing the concern or simply offering solutions, the manager empathizes by saying, "I understand this workload can be overwhelming. Let's discuss how we can balance your tasks to make it more manageable." This response not only shows that the manager has empathy, it also builds trust and fosters a supportive work environment.

Social skills

Social skills encompass effective communication, conflict resolution, collaboration, and the ability to influence and inspire others. Leaders with strong social skills can create positive work environments, foster teamwork, and lead by example. They are effective in leading change and tend to be persuasive. They are also experts at building and leading teams.

A team leader excels in social skills by facilitating open communication among team members, addressing conflicts through constructive dialogue, and inspiring the team to achieve their project goals. These social skills result in improved team morale, efficient problem-solving, and a highly productive work environment.

Let's take the example of Manuel Moreno, an accomplished film producer with a down-to-earth approach and excellent social skills. As a professional in the heart of Hollywood, Antonio is known for his effective people skills and ability for making great films happen. He is the go-to person for getting actors, crew, and scripts all on the same page. When disagreements pop up, he is the cool-headed peacemaker who sorts things out, ensuring the movie stays on course. Outside the set, Antonio is all about building partnerships and connections that help bring films to life. His enthusiasm and leadership inspire everyone he works with, making each project a success.

Using acting to develop emotional intelligence

Although the specific use of acting to foster emotional intelligence and empathic skills has not been widely researched, scholars and practitioners have developed some interesting studies and applications on how fiction can develop empathy. In a literature review conducted by Virginia Libraries, fiction was found to lead to significant changes in readers' worldviews. These changes were attributed to the reader's capacity of transportation into fictional stories and identification with a novel's characters.[5]

In another study, participants read Shaila Abdullah's novel *Saffron Dreams*, which tells the story of a counter-stereotypical Muslim woman in the United States. Then they were asked to determine the race of Arab-Caucasian faces of ambiguous race. When compared to a control group, those who read the novel showed significantly lower race bias towards Arabs by giving more nuanced answers. In a second experiment which was part of the same study, participants were asked to determine the race of ambiguous-race Arab-Caucasian faces showing moderate and high levels of anger. While in the control group higher anger expressions were often associated by participants to Arabs, the bias did not appear in the group that read the novel.[6]

In one class for beginner-level counseling students, the professor developed an activity with the purpose of developing students' empathy toward potential clients through the reading of the first *Harry Potter* book (*Harry Potter and the Sorcerer's Stone*). In this application, empathy was triggered by giving students the opportunity to spend several classes analyzing and discussing how the book's different characters affected the students' views of their clients.[7]

Actors tend to possess high levels of empathy. One study which looked at psychological profiles of professional actors concluded that they have stronger empathetic skills than nonactors.[8] These findings were confirmed by another study that showed that acting increases both empathy and theory of mind, which relates to understanding the states of mind of others.[9] In line with these studies, we will discuss below some acting-based techniques and activities that can be used to develop emotional intelligence in leaders. We will use Goleman's framework to organize the specific goals of the techniques and activities: developing self-awareness, self-regulation, motivation, empathy, and social skills.

Developing self-awareness

In Chapter 4 ("Self-Awareness"), the development of self-awareness is explored through various techniques and insights that draw parallels between acting and leadership. The chapter emphasizes the importance of understanding one's character, feelings, motives, and desires, much like an actor preparing for a role. These skills also apply to the development of self-awareness in the context of emotional intelligence.

One useful technique highlighted in Chapter 4 involves asking the fundamental question, "Who am I?" This question, inspired by the teachings of American acting teacher Uta Hagen, encourages individuals to explore their own life stories, experiences, and beliefs, just like actors do when they approach a role. Leaders are encouraged to reflect on their own life journeys, including both positive and negative experiences, to better understand what drives them as people and leaders.

The chapter also discusses the importance of aligning one's values and beliefs with their actions as a leader. It cites examples such as Satya Nadella, the CEO of Microsoft, who embarked on a journey of self-awareness to transform both himself and the organization he led. His self-reflection led to improvements in empathy, risk-taking, and overall leadership effectiveness.

The case of Anita Roddick, founder of The Body Shop, is also discussed. It illustrates how embracing one's values can lead to groundbreaking business practices, such as ethical consumerism and fair trade. Roddick's self-awareness allowed her to challenge conventional norms and use her business as a force for positive social and environmental change.

Finally, Chapter 4 introduces leadership crucibles as transformative life events that profoundly influence a leader's development. These crucibles provide opportunities for deep self-awareness and the development of empathy. They shape leaders and equip them with valuable lessons for effective leadership. Practical acting-based exercises, such as writing one's autobiography and exploring inner monologues, are particularly useful for identifying leadership crucibles. These exercises are designed to enhance self-awareness by delving into one's life journey, values, beliefs, and emotional responses to various situations.

Developing self-regulation

Developing self-regulation can be facilitated through the application of three acting-based techniques that offer valuable insights and practical tools for individuals aiming to enhance their emotional self-control. These acting-based exercises are belly breathing, which was explained in detail in Chapter 5 ("Presence"); improvisation exercises, which will be discussed in detail in Chapter 9 ("Improvisation and Leadership"); and character analysis.

Belly breathing promotes self-regulation by calming the nervous system and reducing stress responses. This exercise teaches individuals to pause and regain control over their emotions.

Imagine a professional who often faces high-pressure situations in the workplace, such as project deadlines or client meetings. When feeling overwhelmed, they practice deep breathing exercises. Inhaling for a count of four and exhaling for a count of six helps them lower their stress levels and regain composure. This self-regulation technique allows them to approach the situation with a clear mind, make rational decisions, and avoid reacting impulsively. Here is a step-by-step guide to practice belly breathing:

- Begin by selecting a quiet and comfortable space where you won't be easily distracted.
- Sit or lie down in a relaxed position. You can choose to sit in a chair with your feet flat on the floor or lie on your back with your hands resting gently on your abdomen.
- Close your eyes and turn your attention to your breath. Inhale deeply through your nose, allowing your abdomen to rise as you fill your lungs with air. Count to four as you inhale. Exhale slowly and completely through your mouth, counting to six as you release the air. Focus on emptying your lungs entirely.
- Continue this deep breathing exercise for several minutes, concentrating on the rhythm of your breath. Inhale for a count of four and exhale for a count of six. As you breathe deeply, thoughts may arise. Acknowledge them without judgment, and gently bring your focus back to your breath.
- After a few minutes of deep breathing, gradually return your awareness to your surroundings. Open your eyes and sit quietly for a moment before resuming your regular activities.

The second acting-based exercise, the improvisation, can enhance self-regulation by training individuals to adapt and respond thoughtfully to unexpected challenges. It fosters emotional resilience and the ability to maintain composure in unpredictable situations. Consider a team leader who encounters an unexpected crisis during a project presentation. Instead of panicking, they draw on their improvisation skills to handle the situation. They adapt their communication style, address the crisis calmly, and reassure team members. By regulating their emotional response and thinking on their feet, they effectively manage the crisis without escalating tension. Although we will discuss improvisations in detail in Chapter 9, here is an example of an improvisation exercise that can be conducted with a group of participants to develop self-regulation in the context of emotional intelligence:

- Assemble participants in a circle and prepare a list of scenarios or prompts that encourage spontaneous responses. These can range from simple statements to complex scenarios, such as "You've just won the lottery" or "You're stuck in an elevator with a stranger."
- Select a scenario or prompt and present it to the participants. The goal is to encourage immediate, unscripted responses. Participants should respond to the scenario without pre-meditation or planning. Encourage them to fully immerse themselves in the role and react authentically to the given situation.
- Continue to present different scenarios or prompts, allowing participants to explore a range of emotional responses and improvisational skills.
- After each scenario, take a moment for reflection and discussion. Participants can share their experiences, challenges, and insights gained from the exercise. Emphasize the importance of adapting to unexpected situations and remaining composed even when faced with uncertainty.

The last acting-based exercise, character analysis, involves a thoughtful exploration of the emotions, motivations, and triggers experienced by fictional characters in movies or plays. Through this exploration, individuals can gain profound insights into their own emotional triggers and responses, fostering empathy, identification, and self-awareness. This heightened self-awareness becomes a powerful tool for self-regulation, enabling individuals to manage their emotions effectively and make more balanced and thoughtful decisions in their own lives.

Let's consider the character of Forrest Gump from the movie *Forrest Gump*. Forrest is portrayed as a character with a simple and straightforward outlook on life, and he navigates through a series of significant life events with unwavering optimism. Through character analysis, an individual may delve into Forrest's emotional resilience and the way he maintains composure in the face of adversity.

In this analysis, individuals can reflect on how Forrest's ability to remain calm and positive serves as an inspiration. They may identify with their own moments of adversity and explore the emotional triggers that lead them to respond in certain ways. By drawing parallels between Forrest's emotional journey and their own experiences, they can begin to understand their own emotional triggers more deeply. Here's a step-by-step approach on how to do character analysis:

- Choose a fictional character from a movie or play. Ensure that the character's characteristics and experiences resonate with you or mirror aspects of your own emotional landscape. You can use the press reviews to get an idea of who the character is and what their circumstances are.
- Watch the movie or play that features the chosen character, paying close attention to their emotions, reactions, and the events that shape their emotional journey. Take notes on key moments and how the character responds to various situations.
- Reflect on the character's motivations, triggers, and emotional responses. Identify moments in the character's story where they face adversity, challenges, or moments of heightened emotion. Consider how you empathize with the character and what aspects of their emotional journey you relate to.
- Analyze how the character's experiences and emotional triggers parallel your own life situations. Think about times in your life when you faced similar challenges or emotional responses. Identify the emotional triggers that have influenced your own behavior.
- Engage in introspection to deepen your self-awareness. Reflect on your emotional triggers and how they impact your decisions, actions, and relationships. Consider whether there are patterns in your emotional responses that you wish to better understand and regulate.
- Based on your insights from the character analysis and self-reflection, develop self-regulation strategies. These could include techniques such as belly breathing (discussed above), mindfulness, or cognitive reframing (shifting one's

perspective from a negative view to a neutral or positive one) to manage your emotional triggers effectively.

Developing motivation

There is so much actors can teach leaders when it comes to motivation. The passion about their craft that most actors have is truly remarkable. If they were not so motivated and passionate about acting, they would not be able to deal with the difficult demands and high levels of rejection that exist in the acting world.

Actors' dedication, enthusiasm, and love for acting serve as a source of inspiration for others. In the context of emotional intelligence, individuals can draw motivation from observing actors' commitment to their art. This passion-driven motivation can be harnessed to pursue personal and professional goals with enthusiasm and persistence. It encourages individuals to approach their work with a genuine love for what they do. Someone aspiring to become an entrepreneur can draw motivation from the passion actors exhibit for their roles and careers. This enthusiasm can drive them to persevere through the challenges and setbacks involved in leading others.

In addition, actors face frequent rejection throughout their careers. They audition for hundreds of roles but only get a few of them. But they learn to cope with rejection, adapt, and continue pursuing their goals. This resilience can be a valuable lesson for anyone seeking motivation. Learning from the actor's ability to bounce back from setbacks can help individuals overcome discouragement and maintain their drive. It teaches the importance of perseverance and the understanding that setbacks are part of the journey toward success.

Finally, in the process of building a character for a performance, actors often ask themselves, as characters, "What do I want?" This question is a fundamental driver of a character's motivation. Similarly, in the context of emotional intelligence and personal development, leaders can adopt this question to fuel their own motivation. By consistently asking themselves, "What do I want?," they can clarify their goals, desires, and aspirations. This self-reflection helps create a clear sense of purpose, which is a key motivator. When people have a strong sense of what they want to achieve, they are more likely to stay committed and driven to reach their objectives.

Developing empathy

Empathy, as mentioned earlier, is at the core of acting. Every time an actor builds a character for the stage or for a film, they are exercising their empathetic skills since they need to understand who their characters are. The process of building a character inherently involves empathy. It requires actors to put themselves in the shoes of another person.

Leaders wanting to improve their empathetic skills could consciously practice empathy by making an effort to understand the perspectives and feelings of others, in the same way that actors do when they approach a role. They could ask the same questions actors ask themselves about their characters. For example, a manager working in a diverse team can apply the principles of character building by making an effort to understand their colleagues' backgrounds, experiences, and viewpoints. The manager would ask the same questions actors ask in the process of building a character, but about their team members: who are they, what are their circumstances, what are their relationships, what do they want, what are their obstacles, and what do they do to get what they want.

In addition, as mentioned before, Stanislavski's "Magic If" technique encourages actors to ask themselves, "What would I do if I were the character?" This technique transforms the aims of the character into those of the actor, allowing them to connect with the character on a deeper level. Similarly, leaders can adapt this technique to their own lives by considering how they would feel and act if they were in someone else's situation. By exploring the "Magic If" in real-life scenarios, people can develop a heightened sense of empathy and a better understanding of the emotions and reactions of others. A manager facing a conflict within their team can use the "Magic If" technique by imagining themselves in the shoes of each team member involved in the conflict. This exercise can help the manager empathize with their team members' perspectives and work toward a resolution that considers everyone's feelings.

Storytelling, which we covered in Chapter 7 ("Communication"), is also a powerful tool for cultivating empathy. Actors convey the emotions and experiences of their characters through storytelling, allowing the audience to connect with the characters on an emotional level. Both telling stories and actively listening to others' stories can trigger empathy. When individuals share their own stories, they open themselves up to vulnerability, which can foster empathy in those who listen. Additionally, actively listening to others' stories enables individuals to gain insight into the thoughts and feelings of others, deepening their capacity for empathy.

Developing social skills

Although we will cover improvisations in detail in Chapter 9, it is worth mentioning that one of the best ways to develop social skills in the context of emotional intelligence is by participating in improvisation exercises. Improvisation offers a unique and safe environment for individuals to get rid of their inhibitions, overcome shyness, and build social skills. The very essence of improvisation relies on spontaneity, creativity, and taking risks, which can have a profound impact on personal growth and social development.

In addition, improv exercises provide a supportive and non-judgmental space where participants can take risks without the fear of failure or embarrassment. This freedom encourages individuals, including those who may be naturally shy or apprehensive in social situations, to step outside their comfort zones.

Imagine a team-building workshop in a corporate setting where employees are encouraged to engage in improvisation activities. In one exercise, participants are asked to pair up and perform a short skit without any prior preparation. This exercise prompts employees to overcome shyness by taking on new, unexpected roles and interacting with their colleagues in an informal and playful manner. By pushing boundaries and embracing uncertainty, individuals gradually build self-assurance and confidence in their abilities. Success in improv exercises reinforces the notion that taking risks can lead to positive outcomes, a mindset that can be transferred to real-life social interactions.

Conclusion

This chapter explored the concept of emotional intelligence (EQ) as well as the importance of its five components in leadership contexts: self-awareness, self-regulation, motivation, empathy, and social skills. We discussed how the world of acting offers valuable insights and exercises to develop each of the five elements of emotional intelligence. Overall, the chapter provides actionable acting-based strategies for leaders to improve their emotional intelligence and enhance their effectiveness in leading teams.

Reflective questions

1. How do you perceive the role of emotional intelligence in your leadership, and how does it relate to the five components of emotional intelligence identified by Daniel Goleman? Are you better at some components more than others? Which ones?
2. Think about a specific challenging situation you've encountered in your personal or professional life where emotional intelligence played a crucial role. How did your level of emotional intelligence impact the outcome, and what could you have done differently to improve the situation?
3. Can you identify specific instances in your leadership experiences where applying acting-based techniques or exercises could have improved your emotional intelligence and leadership effectiveness?
4. Reflect on a leader or public figure you admire for their strong emotional intelligence. What specific behaviors or qualities do they exhibit that you believe contribute to their high emotional intelligence? How might you incorporate some of these behaviors or qualities into your own leadership style?
5. Imagine a scenario in your workplace where a team is experiencing internal conflicts and reduced productivity due to communication issues. How could the application of improvisation exercises, as discussed in the chapter, help resolve these challenges and improve teamwork and emotional intelligence among team members?

Notes

1 Murphy, K. (2013, April 20). Maya Angelou. *New York Times*, SR2. Retrieve from https://www.nytimes.com/2013/04/21/opinion/sunday /a-chat-with-maya-angelou.html
2 Salovey, P., Mayer, J., & Caruso, D. (2004). Emotional intelligence: Theory, findings, and implications. *Psychological Inquiry*, 15(3), 197–215.
3 Wilson, E. (2015, September). Empathy is still lacking in the leaders who need it most. *Harvard Business Review*. https://hbr.org/2015/09/ empathy-is-still-lacking-in-the-leaders-who-need-it-most
4 Timmins, B. (2021, December 7). Vishal Garg: US boss fires 900 employees over Zoom. *BBC News*. Retrieved from https://www.bbc .com/news/business-59554585
5 Rowe, D. B. (2018). The "novel" approach: Using fiction to increase empathy. *Virginia Libraries*, 63(1).
6 Johnson, D. R., Huffman, B. L., & Jasper, D. M. (2014). Changing race boundary perception by reading narrative fiction. *Basic and Applied Social Psychology*, 36(1), 83–90.
7 Gibson, D. (2007). Empathizing with Harry Potter: The use of popular literature in counselor education. *Journal of Humanistic Counseling, Education and Development*, 46(2), 197–210.
8 Nettle, D. (2006). Psychological profiles of professional actors. *Personality and Individual Differences*, 40, 375–383.
9 Goldstein, T. R. & Winner, E. (2012). Enhancing empathy and theory of mind. *Journal of Cognition and Development*. 13(1), 19–37.

Part III

Performing leadership

In June 2015, just a few weeks after the passing of her husband, Sheryl Sandberg, former chief operating officer of Facebook (now Meta), delivered a commencement speech at Tsinghua University's School of Economics and Management in Beijing, China. In her 20-minute address, she spoke about her husband Dave Goldberg with passion and said "no one won more hearts than my beloved husband." Then she added, "Dave was a truly inspiring leader. He was kind. He was generous. He was thoughtful. He raised the level of performance of everyone around him." During her speech, she stressed that great leaders "do not just want to secure compliance." But rather "they want to elicit genuine enthusiasm, complete trust, and real dedication. They don't just win the minds of their teams, they win their hearts."

Leadership is mainly and foremost about the followers. Those leaders who are able to elevate their followers to the next level, to win their hearts and transform them, are the true performing leaders. Dave Goldberg, founder of LAUNCH Media and CEO of SurveyMonkey, was undoubtedly a very successful business leader, able to create and run world-class companies. However, his real value as a leader was his ability to work with people, to make them grow and to make them better. Goldberg exemplifies the goal we aim to achieve—the ideal of a performing leader.

As we transition from the foundational aspects of leadership explored in Part I and the development of leadership skills through the SPACE model outlined in Part II, we now arrive at Part III: "Performing Leadership." This section shifts our focus to our followers, for whom we have honed our leadership skills throughout this book. Followers are the ones who bring our vision to fruition. We have developed our self-awareness, presence, authenticity,

DOI: 10.4324/9781003349815-11

communication, and emotional intelligence so that we can inspire and guide them toward our shared goals. Here, the curtain rises to explore the art of effective leadership in action.

In Chapter 9, "Improvisation and Leadership," we are going to explore the principles of improvisation as well as different improvisational exercises designed to perform leadership effectively in different leadership contexts. The chapter shows how the art of improvisation can empower leaders to adapt to change, strengthen their social and teamwork skills, and foster creativity and innovation in their followers.

Our final act is Chapter 10 entitled "Leading with Vision." In this chapter, we are going to talk about why having a clear vision is crucial to gain the hearts and support of our followers. We will see how visionary leaders exemplify the five qualities highlighted in the SPACE model: self-awareness, presence, authenticity, communication, and emotional intelligence. We will also take a close look at the case of Indra Nooyi, former CEO of PepsiCo and one of the most remarkable visionary business leaders in recent times. We will conclude by providing a brief summary of the book.

9 Improvisation and leadership

Leaders often say that the only thing that is constant about their work is change. Despite the routines, processes, and procedures they deal with on a daily basis, they tend to find themselves navigating through complex and unpredictable situations. Their ability to adapt, think on their feet, and innovate becomes key for their success.

In acting, the ability to adapt to another actor's performance is one of the most important skills that any actor needs to have if they want their performance to be believable. As part of their training, actors spend many hours doing improvisation exercises to perfect their capacity to adapt. But the benefits of improvisation go beyond adapting; they foster creativity in the actor. As Tina Fey, the American actress and comedian, once said: "In improv there are no mistakes, only beautiful happy accidents. And many of the world's greatest discoveries have been by accident."[1]

Fey reminds us that in improvisation, the unexpected is not to be feared; it needs to be embraced. Mistakes are reframed as opportunities, and spontaneity reigns supreme. In this chapter, we will explore how the spirit of improvisation can serve as a lodestar for leaders as they confront the ever-evolving landscape of leadership challenges.

Before we dive into the specific benefits of improvisation for leadership, let's begin by understanding what improvisation truly is. At its core, improvisation is the art of unscripted performance, where individuals respond to unforeseen challenges and opportunities in the moment. Tina Fey, in her book *Bossypants*, gives us four rules as a solid foundation for understanding how successful improvisations work.

DOI: 10.4324/9781003349815-12

The first rule: Agree (always agree and say yes)

The first rule is simple: always agree and say yes. This means that when a fellow improviser presents an idea or scenario, your response should be one of affirmation and acceptance. By doing so, you build a foundation of trust and collaboration, ensuring that the scene or interaction progresses smoothly. This rule underscores the importance of open-mindedness and receptivity.

Imagine an improvisational scene where one performer initiates a scenario by saying, "We're on a spaceship headed to Mars." The other performer's response of "Yes, and I just spotted an asteroid on our radar" not only affirms the scenario but also contributes to its development.

The second rule: Yes, and (not only to say yes, but yes and)

Building upon the first rule, the second rule of improvisation, "Yes, and," emphasizes not only agreeing with the presented idea but also adding something of your own to enrich the interaction. This rule encourages participants to actively contribute to the conversation and co-create the narrative.

Continuing the spaceship scenario, when the second performer responds with "Yes, and I'm calculating the best course to avoid it," they not only affirm the scenario but also contribute by offering a new element. This approach empowers participants to actively contribute to the conversation and co-create the narrative.

The third rule: Make statements (speak in statements instead of questions)

The third rule of improvisation consists of making statements instead of asking questions. In improvisation, statements drive the narrative forward. By avoiding questions that might stall the scene, improvisers maintain the momentum of the performance. For example, in an improvisation, when one performer states, "We should increase our speed to maneuver around the asteroid," it moves the narrative forward with clarity.

The fourth rule: There are no mistakes

The fourth and final rule of improvisation is a liberating concept: "There are no mistakes." In the world of improv, errors or unexpected developments are not perceived as failures but as opportunities. Participants are encouraged to adapt, embrace the unexpected, and transform perceived mistakes into valuable moments of creativity. For example, in a scene where a performer accidentally drops a prop meant to represent a spaceship control panel, they can embrace it as part of the narrative, improvising around it creatively.

In leadership, this rule carries profound implications. Leaders who embody the there-are-no-mistakes mindset foster an environment where experimentation and calculated risk-taking are encouraged. When a project encounters an unexpected setback, an improvisation-trained leader views it as a chance to learn and innovate, rather than dwelling on perceived failures.

In the following sections, we will explore the intersections of leadership and improvisation in three key leadership scenarios: adapting to change, building effective teams, and fostering creativity and innovation. We will also introduce improvisational exercises tailored to enhance leadership effectiveness in those scenarios.

Adapting to change

Adapting to change is a crucial aspect of leadership. In their seminal work on the subject, Ron Heifetz and Marty Laurie[2] define "adaptive leadership" as a type of leadership that focuses on guiding organizations through systemic, complex challenges that require changes in deeply held beliefs and values. Adaptive leaders need to be flexible. Heifetz and Laurie distinguish six key principles to ensure that a leader can guide their followers through change: maintaining a broad perspective to recognize emerging patterns, accurately identifying the core adaptive challenge, regulating the stress associated with the change, keeping the team focused on critical issues, empowering employees to take responsibility and initiative, and valuing insights from all organizational levels, especially those often overlooked. This approach represents a shift from traditional authoritative leadership to a more collaborative and empowering model, essential for thriving in dynamic business environments.

Improvisation can play a vital role in developing adaptive leaders as it aligns well with the six key principles of adaptive leadership. The following section will analyze how each of the six principles can be developed with improvisation:

1. *Broad perspective*: improvisation fosters out-of-the-box thinking, which contributes to having a broad perspective for recognizing emerging patterns.
2. *Identifying the core adaptive challenge*: improvisation makes participants alert and focused at all times, given that they don't know what is coming. It forces them to always be on their toes and focus on the most critical aspects of the exercise. This practice makes them better at identifying core adaptive challenges.
3. *Managing stress and regulation*: improvisations often involve dealing with uncertainty and pressure, which can help leaders build resilience and composure in high-stress situations. This is a crucial skill for guiding organizations through change.
4. *Keeping the team focus on critical issues*: improvisational exercises often involve problem-solving and decision-making in real-time, training leaders and teams to prioritize and address immediate challenges effectively.
5. *Empowering employees to take initiative*: in improvisation, participants are compelled to take the lead in the exercise because they must respond promptly and adapt in real-time.
6. *Valuing insights from all levels*: adaptive leaders must value insights from all organizational levels, especially those often overlooked. Improvisation aligns with this principle by promoting collaboration and equal participation. This ensures that diverse perspectives are heard and valued.

Improvisation can help develop adaptive leaders by providing practical experiences and skill-building opportunities that align with the core principles of adaptive leadership. It enhances their ability to adapt, manage stress, empower teams, value diverse insights, foster collaboration, and focus on critical issues, making them better equipped to guide people and organizations. Below there are three examples of improvisation exercises designed to enhance skills for adapting to change.

The change initiators

- Gather participants into a circle and explain that the exercise is focused on adapting to change. Provide a basic scenario, such as a team working on launching a flying car.
- Select one participant as the "Change Initiator" and another as the "Inventor-Entrepreneur." The rest of the participants are "Product Team Members."
- Begin the scenario with the Inventor-Entrepreneur discussing the final preparations for the flying car launch with the Product Team Members. As they do this, the Change Initiator unexpectedly introduces a significant change. For example, they might say, "Due to a sudden government regulation change, flying cars can no longer be used for personal transport, and we must pivot to a different market. Your task is to come up with a new and innovative use for our flying car technology."
- The Inventor-Entrepreneur and Product Team Members must adapt to the change quickly and creatively. They must brainstorm and decide on a new market or application for their flying car technology, considering the unexpected regulation shift.
- After the scenario, gather the group and ask participants to share their creative adaptations and innovative ideas for the flying car technology in response to the regulatory change. Discuss different approaches and decisions made.
- Select a new Change Initiator and Inventor-Entrepreneur, and repeat the exercise with a different creative scenario or change introduced by the Change Initiator.
- Summarize the exercise by highlighting the importance of adaptability and creative thinking in responding to unexpected changes in business scenarios, emphasizing how these skills can be applied in real-life leadership and creative problem-solving situations.

Changing roles

- The goal of this exercise is to improve adaptability and flexibility by requiring participants to quickly change their role during a scene.
- Form small groups of participants. Assign each group a scene or scenario (e.g., a job interview, a family dinner, a space mission). Instruct each participant to assume a specific role within the scene.
- Start the scene with a specific scenario or prompt. At random intervals, call out a "change" signal. When the signal is given, participants must quickly switch to a different role within the same scene.
- Continue to call out "change" signals periodically, challenging participants to adapt to new roles and situations while maintaining the scene's continuity.
- Have a discussion with the team to reflect on how they adapted to the changing elements. This exercise helps participants become more comfortable with unexpected changes and adapt to new roles and circumstances, fostering flexibility and adaptability.

Change of genre

- The purpose of this exercise is to practice adaptability by switching between different genres while performing a scene. Divide participants into small groups of three to five people. Each group will be working on their own scene or story.
- Assign each group a starting scene or story with a specific genre. Provide a variety of genres to choose from, such as romantic, action-adventure, horror, comedy, science fiction, fantasy, Western, film noir, etc.
- Give the groups a few minutes to discuss and plan their initial scene or story based on the assigned genre. They should decide on the characters, setting, and basic plot elements.
- Each group performs their initial scene or story for the rest of the participants. They should aim to embody the style and characteristics of the assigned genre as they act out the scene or story. At random intervals during the performance (you can use a timer or call out the changes yourself), announce

a "change of genre" signal. When this signal is given, the groups must immediately switch to a different genre while continuing the scene or story from where they left off.

- Continue the exercise with multiple genre changes, allowing each group to adapt to different styles and tones.
- After the exercise, have a debriefing session with the participants. Discuss their experiences, challenges, and what they learned about adapting to change. Encourage them to share insights on how this exercise can relate to adaptability in real-life situations.

Building effective teams

An effective team is a group where members work together towards a common goal, leveraging their individual skills and expertise. These teams are characterized by clear communication, shared responsibilities, trust among theirmembers, and a strong sense of unity and purpose. They are adaptable, able to resolve conflicts quickly, and have established norms for collaboration. Effective teams also empower their members, allowing for autonomy and decision-making. This results in a more engaged and productive group. Members of effective teams tend to accomplish more as a team rather than individually.

Building an effective team requires three elements: charters, composition, and capacity. They are often referred to as The Three Cs of Effective Teams.[3] The first element, charters, suggests that teams must create contracts that define their operational procedures, members' roles, strategies, and goals. The charter provides clarity and direction for the team members. It also increases accountability as the charter acts as a written contract.

Composition relates to the blend of members' skills, personalities, and experiences, emphasizing the alignment of these attributes with team responsibilities. For a team to be effective, its members' capabilities have to align with the tasks and responsibilities of the team. We need to have the right members, with the right skills, if we want to have an effective team.

Capability focuses on the team's adaptability, driven by members' readiness and ability to adjust to changing circumstances. This adaptability is crucial for navigating challenges and achieving goals. In other words, capability is about how well the team can adapt to unexpected challenges and still work towards achieving its objectives.

Since improvisation fosters a mindset of flexibility and creative thinking, it is an excellent tool to develop capability. When team members engage in improvisations, they become more open to adjusting to the unknown (they ignore what their improvisation partners will say or do). By encouraging team members to think on their feet and make decisions in real-time, improvisation not only helps them adapt to unexpected challenges but also empowers them to explore new perspectives and solutions.

Let's take a look at three improvisation exercises related to building effective teams. The first one fosters capability through storytelling. The second one targets trust among team members. The final one puts participants through a challenge together. It targets key teamwork skills such as collaborating and communicating, solving problems together, and building trust among team members.

The storytellers

- Gather your team in a circle in a comfortable, open space. Explain the purpose of the exercise, emphasizing the importance of adaptability and creative storytelling.
- Begin with one team member by having them start telling a simple story with a single sentence. For example, "Once upon a time, there was a curious boy." Then, the team member to their right adds the next sentence to the story, and the story continues around the circle with each member adding one sentence at a time.
- Encourage team members to be imaginative and creative with their contributions, building upon the narrative in unexpected ways.
- At random intervals (determined by you or another team member), introduce a new element or challenge into the story. This could be a change in setting, a character twist, an unexpected event, or a change in tone. When a new element is introduced, the storytellers must adapt the story accordingly, seamlessly incorporating the change into the ongoing narrative.

- After a set period, conclude the exercise and have a discussion with the team to reflect on how they adapted to the changing elements, how they maintained the flow of the story, and what they learned about working together in an improvisational context.

The trust circle

- The purpose of this exercise is to build trust within a team. Have the team form a circle, standing close together. Ask one team member to step into the center of the circle, blindfolded. This person will be the "trustee."
- The remaining team members will be the "spotters" standing around the circle. Their job is to guide and protect the trustee.
- The trustee should stand still with their arms crossed over their chest, blindfolded, and completely passive.
- Instruct the spotters to take turns gently guiding the trustee around the circle, using only their fingertips on the trustee's shoulders. They can talk to them in the guiding process. The objective is for the spotters to guide the trustee safely around the circle without letting them stumble or fall. You can introduce obstacles, like a chair, to make it more challenging.
- The trustee should focus on trusting their teammates and following their guidance.
- After each round, rotate roles so that each team member has a chance to be the trustee and the spotters.
- Emphasize the importance of clear and effective communication among the spotters and the trustee. This exercise encourages participants not only to trust each other, but also to be able to communicate effectively.
- After the exercise, have a discussion about the importance of trust and effective communication in the workplace. Encourage participants to share their experiences and what they learned about teamwork and trust.

The human knot

- Gather the team in a circle, standing close together, shoulder to shoulder, and facing the center of the circle.

- Instruct each team member to extend their right hand and reach across the circle to grasp the right hand of someone standing across from them. Simultaneously, they should extend their left hand and reach across to hold the left hand of a different person across from them. Each person should be holding hands with two different people, creating a "knot" of interconnected arms. Participants should avoid holding hands with the people standing directly next to them, as this will make the exercise more challenging.
- Once everyone has their hands joined, explain the objective of the exercise: the team must work together to untangle themselves without breaking the handholds or letting go of anyone's hands.
- Encourage participants to communicate effectively to find a solution. They communicate to plan their movements and coordinate with their fellow team members.
- Participants should step over, under, and around each other as needed to achieve the goal of forming a complete circle while still holding hands.
- Remind the group that they must not let go of anyone's hands during the process. If someone accidentally lets go, the group must start over. The team can work together, test different approaches, and collaborate to find a way to untangle the knot.
- Once the group successfully forms a complete circle without breaking any handholds, the exercise is considered complete. After the exercise, have a debriefing session where the team discusses what they learned working together, communication, and trust.
- The "Human Knot" exercise challenges participants to work together closely, communicate effectively, and trust each other to achieve a common objective. It promotes teamwork, problem-solving, and a sense of unity among team members.

Fostering creativity and innovation

In a business context, we make a clear distinction between creativity and innovation. Creativity is mainly about generating ideas. Innovation, on the other hand, refers to both the creation of ideas and their implementation. Creativity is thought of as being more connected with the initial stages of the innovation process. This means that while creativity is about coming up with new and novel ideas, innovation extends to the practical application of those ideas. Thus, innovation involves activities such as finding the right resources, coming up with the actual invention, and introducing it to the market.

Improvisation offers many benefits for fostering creativity and innovation. At its core, improvisation is a creative activity. It encourages participants to come up with new ideas and solutions in real time. It also promotes risk-taking and out-of-the-box thinking, which are key traits in the creative process.

In addition, improvisation generally involves working with others in a team. This collaborative aspect is also important for fostering innovation. It also helps individuals become better communicators, both verbally and non-verbally. Effective communication is crucial for developing innovative ideas within a team and sharing them with others.

Finally, improvisation often involves making mistakes and learning from them. It helps participants become more comfortable with failure. This is an inherent part of innovation because it leads to more experimentation and risk-taking behavior in the creation process. Below we will present three different improvisation exercises aimed at fostering creativity and innovation.

Creating a new product together

- Gather a group of participants. Explain to the group that this improvisation is about coming up with a new and innovative product. Tell them that the first person will need to start with the sentence: "I think we should create a new product for ..."
- Have the first person finish the sentence. For example, they could say "I think we should create a new product for travelers."
- The next person responds with "Yes, and ..." and builds upon the previous idea. For example, "Yes, and it should be a smartphone app that helps travelers find unique local experiences."
- Each subsequent participant continues the "Yes, and ..." pattern, adding new ideas or details to the concept. For example, "Yes, and it should have a feature that connects

travelers with local guides who can offer personalized recommendations."

- The key is to encourage participants to accept and build upon each other's ideas without judgment or negativity. This exercise promotes a collaborative and open-minded atmosphere where innovative ideas can flourish. It helps participants think creatively, explore possibilities, and come up with innovative solutions by building upon the contributions of others.

Object transformation

- Gather a group of participants and provide them with a random object. It could be anything, such as a rubber duck, a paperclip, a spoon, or a stuffed animal.
- The first participant takes the object and comes up with a creative and unconventional use for it that somewhat corresponds to its characteristics. For example, if the object is a rubber duck, they might say, "this rubber duck can be a microphone for singing in the shower."
- After sharing their idea, the first participant passes the object to the next person in the circle. The next participant takes the object and comes up with a completely different and imaginative use for it. For instance, if they receive the rubber duck, they might say, "now, this rubber duck transforms into a secret compartment for hiding small valuables."
- Continue passing the object around the circle, with each participant providing a new, creative use for it. Encourage participants to think outside the box and embrace the absurd and unexpected. The goal is to explore the object's potential in unconventional ways.
- This exercise encourages participants to think creatively. It makes connections between unrelated concepts, and challenges their assumptions about everyday objects. It can be a fun and engaging way to stimulate innovative thinking and inspire participants to view objects and problems from different angles.

Product mashup

- The goal of this exercise is to stimulate creative thinking and innovation by combining elements from different products to create a new and unique concept.
- Gather participants in a circle. Write down the names of various everyday objects, products, or technologies on separate pieces of paper (e.g., toaster, bicycle, smartphone, umbrella, blender, camera). Place these pieces of paper in a container.
- Ask each participant to draw one piece of paper from the container, revealing the name of the product they've selected.
- Instruct participants to imagine how they can combine the features, functions, or characteristics of the product they drew with the product or technology of the person sitting to their right. They should aim to create a completely new and innovative product concept.
- Ask each participant to present their product mashup to the group, explaining how it works, its unique features, and the problem it solves. Remind participants to think creatively and explore unconventional combinations of products and technologies.
- After all presentations, open the floor for questions, feedback, and discussions. Encourage participants to ask questions, provide constructive feedback, and discuss the innovative aspects of each concept.

Conclusion

This chapter explored the connection between improvisation and leadership, and discussed four foundational rules of improvisation: "Always Agree and Say Yes," "Yes, And," "Make Statements," and "There Are No Mistakes." In addition, the chapter explored three key leadership qualities and showed how they can be developed through improvisation: adapting to change, working well with others, and fostering creativity and innovation. Finally, the chapter provided three different improvisation exercises for each of the three leadership qualities discussed.

Reflective questions

1. How can the four foundational rules of improvisation ("Always Agree and Say Yes," "Yes, And," "Make Statements," "There Are No Mistakes") be integrated into your leadership style to foster a more open and creative work environment?

2. Reflect on a recent leadership challenge you encountered that required adaptation to change. How might the principles of adaptive leadership, such as broadening perspective or managing stress, have helped you navigate that situation more effectively?

3. Recall a recent significant change or challenge your organization faced. If you were to implement improvisation exercises such as "The Change Initiator," "Changing Roles," and "Change of Genre" to address similar changes in the future, in what order would you introduce these exercises, and why?

4. Think about a recent team collaboration within your organization. If you wanted to enhance trust, communication and collaboration among team members, in which order, and why, would you introduce the improvisation exercises focused on building effective teams ("The Storytellers," "The Trust Circle," and "The Human Knot")?

5. Reflect on a recent situation where your team or organization needed to foster creativity and innovation to solve a problem or explore new opportunities. If you were to introduce the improvisation exercises presented in the chapter, such as "Creating a new product together," "Object transformation," and "Product mashup," in what order and why would you use these exercises to inspire and develop innovative thinking in your team members for future challenges?

Notes

1   Fey, T. (2011). *Bossypants*. Little, Brown & Company.
2   Heifetz R. A., Laurie D. L. (1997, Jan–Feb). The work of leadership. *Harvard Business Review*, 75(1), 124–134. PMID: 10174450.
3   Kinicki, A. (2021). *Organizational Behavior*. (3rd ed.). Mc Graw Hill.

10 Leading with vision

Oscar Wilde, the 19th-century Irish playwright and poet, is known around the world for his witty lines. One good example of his humor is this line from the play, *Lady Windermere's Fan*. In Act III, Lord Darlington states, "We are all in the gutter, but some of us are looking at the stars."[1] In the scene, Lord Darlington reflects on women's opinions of men. "They always do find us bad," he says in the previous line.

Although Wilde's line has nothing to do with leadership, it gives a valuable leadership lesson by contrasting the metaphorical "gutter" of flawed, earthly existence with the aspirational gaze towards the "stars" of ideals and dreams. In leadership, like in life, it is important to acknowledge the challenges and difficulties we face while also envisioning the potential for beauty and greatness.

During the COVID-19 pandemic, we were all in the gutter, facing unprecedented challenges. We were in need of leaders with vision, looking at the stars, to open our eyes and show us the beauty beyond the catastrophe. Leaders who knew that things were going to get better, who were sure that it was not the end of the world. Leaders like Jacinda Ardern, discussed in Chapter 1, the former prime minister of New Zealand, who guided her country with assurance and empathy throughout the pandemic. COVID, in a way, was the ultimate leadership test.

Yet, leadership is not only tested by global pandemics; it is an ongoing process, challenged by everyday obstacles. In this closing chapter, we will discuss the importance of vision as a fundamental trait of effective leadership. We will explore what a visionary leader is, and will unveil how a visionary leader embodies every element of the SPACE model: self-awareness, presence, authenticity, communication skills, and emotional intelligence. We will

DOI: 10.4324/9781003349815-13

also look at the case of Indra Nooyi, former CEO of PepsiCo, one of the most prominent visionary leaders in business. The chapter will end with a summary of the book.

Visionary leadership

The term "vision" can encompass a range of meanings, including the act or power of seeing, the ability to imagine or plan for the future, and even mystical or supernatural sights. It also refers to the sense by which objects' qualities are perceived, such as their color, shape, and size, through a process where light rays entering the eye are transformed into signals that pass to the brain.[2]

Vision is not merely a vague idea but a well-defined and inspiring destination. For example, consider the vision of Martin Luther King Jr. during the Civil Rights Movement in the United States. His famous "I have a dream" speech articulated a vision of a future where racial equality would be a reality, inspiring count-less individuals to work towards that goal.[3]

A strong leadership vision also involves the ability to set spe-cific goals and objectives that lead towards the desired future state. Leaders need to outline a roadmap for achieving the vision, breaking it down into actionable steps. For instance, in the world of technology, Elon Musk's vision for SpaceX is to make human-ity a multi-planetary species. To achieve this vision, he has set specific objectives like developing reusable rockets and establish-ing a colony on Mars.[4]

Visionary leadership is about painting a vivid picture of what success looks like, even when the present may seem gloomy. Visionary leaders give their teams something to strive for, some-thing worth overcoming obstacles for. They infuse hope into their organizations, instilling a sense of purpose that extends beyond immediate challenges. In essence, they create a shared vision that becomes a driving force for their team's efforts.

In a leadership context, vision and visionary leadership have long been recognized as crucial elements in leading followers towards success. Burt Nanus, a renowned expert in the field of leadership and management, has made significant contributions to our understanding of these concepts. In his book *Visionary Leadership: Creating a Compelling Sense of Direction for Your Organization,*[5] Nanus highlights that a vision represents a clear and inspiring picture of what an organization or an individual hopes to achieve in the long term. It is not merely a statement of goals or objectives, but a vivid and compelling description of the desired future state.

One of the key characteristics of visionary leadership is the ability to create a shared vision. Visionary leaders do not impose their vision on others but instead involve their team members in the vision-building process. They seek input and feedback, fostering a sense of ownership and commitment among their followers. By involving others in shaping the vision, visionary leaders ensure that it resonates with the values and aspirations of the entire organization.

Furthermore, Nanus highlights the role of persistence and resilience in visionary leadership. Achieving a compelling vision often involves facing challenges and setbacks. Visionary leaders are determined and resilient, willing to persevere in the face of adversity. They maintain their focus on the long-term goals and remain committed to the vision, even when obstacles seem insurmountable.

Nanus emphasizes the importance of flexibility and adaptability in visionary leadership. While the core vision remains unchanged, visionary leaders are open to adjusting strategies and tactics as circumstances evolve. They are willing to embrace change and innovation, ensuring that the organization can navigate the complexities of a dynamic environment while staying true to its long-term vision.

Integrating the SPACE model with Burt Nanus' concepts of visionary leadership can provide a comprehensive framework for developing visionary leaders, who can effectively articulate, share, and guide their organizations towards a compelling future vision. Here's how each component of the SPACE model can be applied to develop and enhance visionary leadership.

Self-awareness

Self-aware leaders are more capable of understanding their strengths, weaknesses, values, and beliefs which is crucial for crafting a vision that is authentic. This self-knowledge enables leaders to articulate their purpose and to be more confident and convincing when communicating their vision. Self-awareness, which is based on the question "Who am I?," the same question actors asked themselves when creating their characters, allows leaders to ensure their vision reflects their true self. Self-awareness makes their visions more resonant and compelling for their followers, in the same way an audience is more impacted when the actor knows and understands their character well.

Presence

In the context of leadership, presence refers to the leader's ability to be fully engaged and attentive in the moment, creating a strong and influential aura. This helps in effectively communicating the vision and engaging with followers on a deeper level. Enhancing presence through acting techniques, as seen in Chapter 5, allows leaders to command attention and convey their vision more powerfully. It involves not just physical presence but also the ability to connect emotionally and intellectually with their followers, making the vision more persuasive.

Authenticity

Authenticity involves being genuine and true to one's values and beliefs. For visionary leaders, authenticity ensures that the vision they propose is not only believable but also that it inspires trust and loyalty in their followers. By being authentic, leaders ensure that their vision and their leadership style match their true self, which fosters trust and inspiration. Acting techniques, as seen in Chapter 6, allow leaders be able to express who they truly are. Thus, they are perceived as more credible and relatable, which can significantly enhance the impact of their vision among their followers.

Communication skills

Effective communication is essential for visionary leaders to articulate and share their vision clearly, so that they can inspire others. This includes not only verbal communication but also non-verbal cues and the ability to listen and adapt messages to different audiences. Developing advanced communication skills through acting techniques enables leaders to present their vision in a way that is engaging, clear, and adaptable to the audience's needs and feedback. It also helps in negotiating, persuading, and involving others in the vision-building process. Visionary leaders can use storytelling and persuasive techniques to make the vision come alive for their team members, inspiring them to strive for excellence and overcome obstacles.

Emotional intelligence

Emotional intelligence involves understanding and managing one's emotions and those of others. For a visionary leader, emotional intelligence is crucial in connecting with followers on an emotional level, fostering a shared vision. Actors, whose job is to put themselves in the shoes of their characters, develop empathy through their training. As seen in Chapter 8, this training is equally useful for leaders to foster their emotional intelligence in general and empathy in particular. Leaders with high emotional intelligence can effectively foster a positive and supportive environment. This is vital for maintaining morale and motivation, especially when the path towards the vision involves obstacles.

Incorporating the SPACE model into the development of visionary leadership allows for a holistic approach that not only focuses on the cognitive aspects of crafting and communicating a vision but also emphasizes the emotional and relational dynamics essential for inspiring and leading a team towards a shared future. This approach aligns with and enhances Nanus' principles by ensuring that the vision is not only compelling and well-communicated but also deeply connected to the leader's authentic self and resonant with the team's values and aspirations. Now let's review the case of Indra Nooyi, an exemplary visionary leader.

The case of Indra Nooyi: A visionary leader

The case of Indra Nooyi, PepsiCo's CEO from 2006 to 2018, is one of the best examples of what visionary leaders can accomplish for their followers and organizations. After taking control of the American food and beverage company in 2006, she was credited for changing the company's strategic direction by increasing corporate expenditures in healthier products, including soft drinks without aspartame, yogurts with more fruits, and potato chips with less sodium. In 2015, under her leadership, the company's net revenue grew 14% to $66 billion. Major publications like *Forbes* and *Fortune* have ranked her among the most powerful business women in the world. She published her memoir, *My Life in Full*, in 2021,[6] in which she tells her journey from her childhood in India to becoming one of the world's most admired CEOs and the first woman of color and immigrant to run a Fortune 50 company.

A native of the Indian city of Madras, known today as Chennai, Nooyi graduated with a degree in physics, chemistry, and mathematics from Madras Christian College and received a postgraduate diploma in management from the Indian Institute of Management in Calcutta. Later on, she obtained a master's degree in public and private management from the Yale School of Management. Before starting her career with PepsiCo in 1994, Nooyi held managerial positions at Asea Brown Boveri, Motorola, and the Boston Consulting Group.

Indra Nooyi is widely regarded as a visionary leader for her transformative impact on PepsiCo, and for her broader influence on corporate leadership and sustainability practices.[7] Her visionary status while being PepsiCo's CEO is underscored by the following five aspects: her visionary strategic reorientation of the company's business, her focus on sustainability and corporate social responsibility, her global perspective and focus on diversity, her focus on innovation, and her influence beyond PepsiCo. In addition, her 5 Cs leadership model, which is covered at the end of this case, has become the preferred leadership framework of many current and aspiring leaders.

Visionary strategic reorientation

Nooyi repositioned PepsiCo's portfolio towards healthier products, anticipating the shift in consumer preferences towards wellness and nutrition long before it became a general trend. Under her leadership, PepsiCo acquired companies in the health and wellness space, including Tropicana and Quaker Oats, and significantly expanded its product lineup to include more nutritious snacks and beverages. This strategic reorientation not only diversified PepsiCo's offerings but also aligned the company with future market trends, ensuring long-term growth and sustainability.

Sustainability and corporate responsibility

Recognizing the importance of sustainability and corporate social responsibility, Nooyi launched the "Performance with Purpose" initiative, which aimed to integrate societal contribution into PepsiCo's core business strategy. This initiative focused on delivering sustainable growth by investing in a healthier future for people and the planet. It included goals related to nutrition, environmental sustainability, and employee well-being. Nooyi's emphasis on sustainability set a precedent in the industry, showcasing how large corporations can thrive while making positive contributions to society and the environment.

As a result of her initiative, PepsiCo's products are now classified into three categories defined by their level of healthiness: (1) "Good for you," which consists of nutritious products such as fruits, vegetables, grains, and other healthy products. (2) "Fun for you," which includes the traditional food and beverages associated with the brand such as soft drinks and potato chips. And (3) "Better for you," which consists of an array of snacks and beverages with fewer or zero calories than the "Fun for you" products.

Global perspective and focus on diversity

As an Indian citizen having worked across the globe, Nooyi brought a unique global perspective to her leadership role at PepsiCo. She leveraged her deep understanding of diverse markets to drive PepsiCo's expansion into emerging markets, which was crucial for the American company's global growth strategy. Nooyi's ability to navigate cultural nuances and adapt strategies to local markets has been a hallmark of her visionary leadership.

Nooyi is also celebrated for her commitment to diversity, equity, and inclusion. As one of the few female executives in the highly competitive food and beverage industry, she was a role model and advocate for women in leadership. Nooyi has spoken extensively on the importance of diversity in decision-making processes and has worked to promote leadership opportunities for women and underrepresented groups within PepsiCo and beyond.

Focus on innovation

Nooyi fostered a culture of innovation within PepsiCo, encouraging the development of new products and the adoption of innovative technologies and business practices. This focus on innovation was not limited to product development but extended to all areas of the business, including manufacturing, marketing, and distribution. Her leadership in innovation ensured that PepsiCo remained competitive in a rapidly changing global marketplace.

Influence beyond PepsiCo

Indra Nooyi's influence extends beyond her tenure at PepsiCo. She has been a prominent voice on global business issues, including economic growth, climate change, and public health. Her insights and leadership have earned her spots on various boards and influential forums where she continues to advocate for responsible business practices and strategic leadership.

Nooyi's remarkable journey from a small town in India to becoming one of the most powerful and admired female CEOs in the world has inspired countless women to pursue leadership roles. As mentioned earlier, Nooyi has also been a vocal advocate for diversity and inclusion throughout her career. Her efforts to promote diversity within PepsiCo and other organizations have set a precedent for inclusive leadership. Nooyi's influence in this regard extends to her participation in discussions and initiatives aimed at breaking down barriers for underrepresented groups in various industries.

Nooyi's commitment to sustainability, as mentioned above, extends to a global scale. She has been a prominent voice in conversations about climate change and corporate responsibility. Her leadership in promoting sustainable practices within PepsiCo, such as reducing water usage and plastic waste, has had a positive ripple effect throughout the business world. Her influence encourages other leaders and organizations to prioritize sustainability and contribute to a more eco-conscious future.

Beyond the business arena, Indra Nooyi has actively engaged in discussions on public policy and global affairs. Her insights and experiences have made her a sought-after voice in international forums and think tanks. She co-chaired the World Economic

Forum in 2008. Her perspectives on economic growth, trade, and global cooperation have contributed to shaping important dialogues on pressing global challenges.

In addition, Indra Nooyi's commitment to education and mentorship underscores her dedication to nurturing future leaders. She has shared her wisdom and experiences with thousands of students and aspiring professionals around the world. In fact, in 2022, she delivered a keynote speech at my institution, the USC Marshall School of Business. Her mentorship has empowered individuals to develop their leadership skills and pursue their goals with confidence.

Indra Nooyi's influence goes well beyond her role as a CEO. She has become a symbol of visionary leadership, gender equality, and responsible corporate citizenship. Her advocacy for diversity, sustainability, and education has left an indelible mark on the world. She has inspired individuals and organizations alike to strive for excellence and make a positive impact on society. As the *Financial Times* puts it, if there was a Nobel Prize for management, Indra Nooyi would be a nominee.[8]

Indra Nooyi's leadership model

When asked about her success, Nooyi often speaks about her Five Cs to Leadership,[9] a model that she has adopted throughout her life. We briefly mentioned this model in Chapter 8.

The first C, *competency*, refers to the leader's ability to excel at something. This, she says, requires leaders to be life-long learners, always willing to refine their knowledge of their chosen field, so that they can remain ahead of everything that goes on in that field.

Her second C is a pair consisting of both *courage and confidence*. This is related to the leader's audacity to speak out so that their knowledge can be demonstrated and shared with others.

The third C is *communication skills*. In this respect, she says: "you cannot overinvest in communication skills, both written and oral, because as a leader you have to constantly mobilize the troops."

The fourth C is *consistency*. She stresses that this does not mean that leaders cannot change their minds, but that changes need to happen within a consistent framework so that followers do not have to second-guess the leader's decisions.

The fifth and final C is *compass*, which deals with the leader's integrity and moral values. In this respect, Nooyi says: "if you don't have integrity, that compass doesn't point true north. Everything comes crashing down as we've seen in recent times."

Indra Nooyi's tenure as CEO of PepsiCo stands as an example of the profound impact visionary leadership can have on an organization. Her strategic vision, commitment to sustainability and corporate social responsibility, and emphasis on diversity and innovation have not only transformed PepsiCo into a more health-conscious and globally competitive company, but have also redefined the role of business in society. Nooyi's story illustrates the power of visionary leadership to drive change, inspire growth, and make a lasting impact on both the organization and the wider world.

Conclusion

This book has taken a unique perspective on leadership, one that I believe has the potential to reshape the way we think about leadership in general, and the way we develop leadership skills in particular. It brings together the worlds of leadership and acting, two seemingly different fields, and shows us how they are remarkably interconnected. The book is based on the idea that leadership is not just about managing people or achieving goals. Leadership is a performance, an art form in itself aimed at inspiring followers to achieve a common goal. Just as actors bring characters to life on stage, leaders have the power to inspire and influence their teams, creating a meaningful impact.

Part I sets the stage by drawing inspiration from Warren Bennis, a pioneer in leadership studies. For Bennis, leadership is an art that requires creativity, intuition, and the ability to adapt, much like the work of a musician or a dancer. Effective leadership goes beyond achieving goals; it involves expressing one's identity and values authentically.

The SPACE model which was introduced in Part II, "Building the Leadership Role," simplifies the complexities of leadership into five essential qualities: self-awareness, presence, authenticity, communication, and emotional intelligence. These qualities are not just abstract concepts but practical skills that leaders can develop and refine through acting techniques and exercises. They also offer a structured roadmap for leadership development.

Throughout the book, we explored the world of acting techniques, from Stanislavski's Method to Hagen's "Inner Objects." We looked at how these techniques, originally designed for actors, can be applied to leadership. We showed how they provide leaders with tools to express authenticity, tap into their emotions, and connect with their teams at a deeper level.

In Part III, "Performing Leadership," we shifted the focus to the followers. The exploration of improvisation opened up new possibilities for developing our own leadership skills and those of others. It showed us how embracing uncertainty, collaborating effectively, and fostering innovation can be cultivated through improvisation. We also looked at the power of visionary leadership and how it embodies the SPACE qualities. The case of Indra Nooyi demonstrated how a visionary leader can impact not only their own followers and organization but also the world at large.

In conclusion, this book challenges us to view leadership as a performance. It encourages current and future leaders to step into the "empty space" armed with the skills of self-awareness, presence, authenticity, communication, and emotional intelligence. It invites us to improvise and take risks, to be like actors, to connect with our teams on a deeper level, and to lead with vision. This book not only provides valuable insights but also inspires us to become better leaders in our own unique way. As stated by Howard Schultz, former CEO of Starbucks known for his charismatic and passionate leadership:

> Leadership is like theater, and you're always on stage. You have to be authentic, you have to be real, and you have to be able to communicate in a way that moves people.[10]

Reflective questions

1. How can the concept of visionary leadership, as discussed in this chapter, be applied to your current leadership role or future leadership aspirations?
2. Reflect on the qualities and attributes of Indra Nooyi as a visionary leader. Which aspects of her leadership style and

strategies resonate with you the most, and how might you incorporate them into your own leadership approach?

3. Think about a challenging situation or project within your organization. How can you apply the principles of visionary leadership, as discussed in this chapter, to inspire your team and guide them toward a shared vision for overcoming the challenges and achieving success?

4. Visionary leaders often face challenges and obstacles on their journey. Can you recall a personal or professional situation where you had to demonstrate resilience and adaptability in pursuit of a visionary goal? What did you learn from that experience?

5. Reflect on Indra Nooyi's advocacy for diversity, sustainability, and corporate responsibility. In what ways can you promote these values within your organization or community, and how might they contribute to your vision as a leader?

Notes

1 Wilde, O. (1985). "We are all in the gutter, but some of us are looking at the stars." In *The Importance of Being Earnest and Other Plays*. Signet Classic: New York.
2 Merriam-Webster. (n.d.). Vision. In Merriam-Webster.com dictionary. Retrieved February 2, 2024, from https://www.merriam-webster.com/dictionary/vision
3 King, M. L., Jr. (1963, August 28). I have a dream. National Archives.
4 SpaceX (2024, February). Mission. Retrieved from https://www.spacex.com/mission/
5 Nanus, B. (1992). *Visionary Leadership: Creating a Compelling Sense of Direction for Your Organization*. Jossey-Bass.
6 Nooyi, I. (2021). *My Life in Full: Work, Family, and Our Future*. Portfolio/Penguin.
7 Ignatius, Adi (2015, September 2015). How Indra Nooyi turned design thinking into strategy: An interview with PepsiCo's CEO. *Harvard Business Review*. https://hbr.org/2015/09/how-indra-nooyi-turned-design-thinking-into-strategy
8 Hill, Andrew (2019, October 13). The nominee for a Nobel Prize for management. https://www.ft.com/content/2616da8c-eb62-11e9-85f4-d00e5018f061
9 Nooyi, Indra (2011). Five Cs of Leadership. https://www.youtube.com/watch?v=u0DMaydBOxk (accessed on 25 January 2024).
10 Schultz, H., & Yang, J. (2012). *Onward: How Starbucks Fought for Its Life without Losing Its Soul*. New York, NY: Rodale Books.

Index

For Product Safety Concerns and Information please contact our EU
representative GPSR@taylorandfrancis.com
Taylor & Francis Verlag GmbH, Kaufingerstraße 24, 80331 München, Germany

www.ingramcontent.com/pod-product-compliance
Lightning Source LLC
Chambersburg PA
CBHW070346270326
41926CB00017B/4017